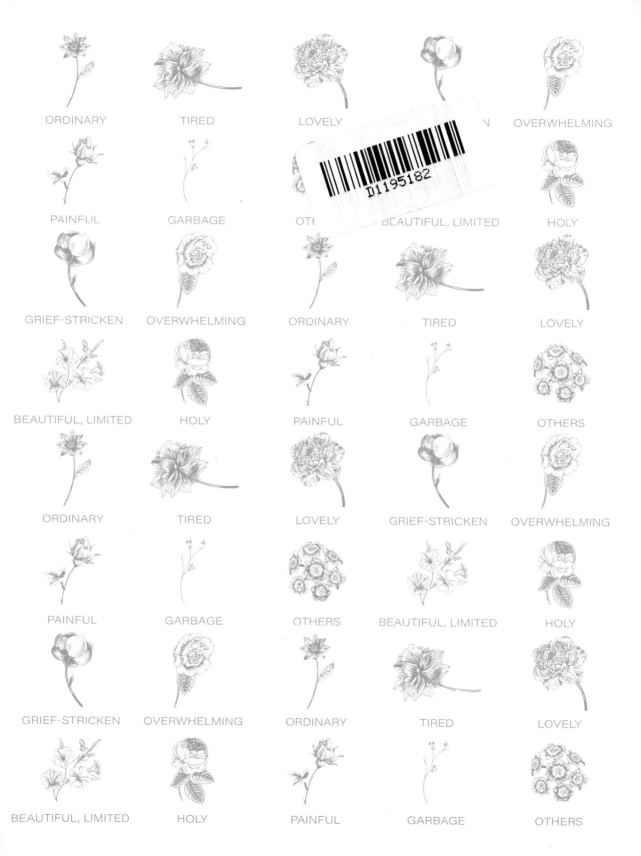

ORDINARY

TIRED

LOVELY

OVERWHELMING

PAINFUL

GARBAGE

BEAUTIFUL, LIMITED

HOLY

GRIEF-STRICKEN

OVERWHELMING

ORDINARY

TIRED

LOVELY

BEAUTIFUL, LIMITED

HOLY

PAINFUL

GARBAGE

OTHERS

ORDINARY

TIRED

LOVELY

GRIEF-STRICKEN

OVERWHELMING

PAINFUL

GARBAGE

OTHERS

BEAUTIFUL, LIMITED

HOLY

GRIEF-STRICKEN

OVERWHELMING

ORDINARY

TIRED

LOVELY

BEAUTIFUL, LIMITED

HOLY

PAINFUL

GARBAGE

OTHERS

BY KATE BOWLER AND JESSICA RICHIE

The Lives We Actually Have: 100 Blessings for Imperfect Days

Good Enough: 40ish Devotionals for a Life of Imperfection

BY KATE BOWLER

No Cure for Being Human (And Other Truths I Need to Hear)

The Preacher's Wife: The Precarious Power of Evangelical Women Celebrities

Everything Happens for a Reason (And Other Lies I've Loved)

Blessed: A History of the American Prosperity Gospel

THE
LIVES WE
ACTUALLY
HAVE

THE LIVES WE ACTUALLY HAVE

100 Blessings for Imperfect Days

Kate Bowler and Jessica Richie

CONVERGENT
NEW YORK

Published in the United States by Convergent Books,
an imprint of Random House, a division of
Penguin Random House LLC, New York.

CONVERGENT BOOKS is a registered trademark and its C colophon
is a trademark of Penguin Random House LLC.

LIBRARY OF CONGRESS CATALOGING-IN-PUBLICATION DATA
Names: Bowler, Kate, author. | Richie, Jessica, author.
Title: The lives we actually have / Kate Bowler, and Jessica Richie.
Description: First edition. | New York : Convergent, 2023
Identifiers: LCCN 2022036799 (print) | LCCN 2022036800 (ebook) |
ISBN 9780593193709 (hardcover) | ISBN 9780593193716 (ebook)
Subjects: LCSH: Gratitude—Quotations, maxims, etc. | Spiritual life. | Meditations. |
Aphorisms and apothegms.
Classification: LCC BJ1533.G8 B65 2023 (print) | LCC BJ1533.G8 (ebook) |
DDC 179/.9—dc23/eng/20221007
LC record available at https://lccn.loc.gov/2022036799
LC ebook record available at https://lccn.loc.gov/2022036800

PRINTED IN THE UNITED STATES OF AMERICA ON ACID-FREE PAPER

crownpublishing.com

6th Printing

First Edition

Book design by Elizabeth Rendfleisch

Kate:

Mom, you taught me to bless the day.
Your early morning faith is a wonder,
even though it makes you have to go to bed at roughly 7 PM.

Jessica:

For my (not so) little sisters.
Any courage I have, I borrowed from the four of you.
You have gotten me through my best and worst and most mediocre of days.
How lucky am I to have your DNA woven in mine?

Contents

BLESS THIS *LOVELY* LIFE

BLESS THIS *GRIEF-STRICKEN* LIFE

BLESS THIS *OVERWHELMING* LIFE

BLESS THIS *PAINFUL* LIFE

BLESS THIS *GARBAGE* LIFE

BLESS THE LIVES OF *OTHERS*

BLESS THIS *BEAUTIFUL, LIMITED* LIFE

BLESS THIS *HOLY* LIFE

Introduction

BLESS THESE DAYS

I f we are very lucky, we have days lit up with fireworks. We have powerful moments of connection—to the world, to each other, and even to God—that dazzle us. Suddenly, beauty and possibility are everywhere. We thought we were living any old day, but no. We find ourselves amazed by truths we didn't set out to learn.

Some days steer us straight toward the divine. It is a March morning and the dogwood tree outside my window has exploded into so many white blooms that it looks like it slipped into a wedding dress overnight. And I remember that creation is conspiring to fill me with awe. (And interrupt my productivity. If I stay in my air-conditioned office all day, I can avoid gratitude for God's creation altogether and finally empty my inbox, *praise God*.)

Or I might find an evening that wraps me up in familial peace. The television is buzzing, and my father and I are curled up on the couch, my head resting on his warm stomach to feel the slow rise and fall of his breath. Inhale, exhale. We are feeling any space between us evaporate into the very air we breathe.

Usually there is no way to predict whether our days and our nights will offer us much of anything. Except that, every now and again, we find a normal (probably boring) night turns around in an instant. It is late in the evening, and I am in a shuttle bus full of polite colleagues. There is not much chatter until someone hears the first notes of a familiar song played on the radio and then, there we are, yelling the chorus with unearned confidence.

Nothing is more powerful for me than the moment latent in each day when I feel the rainbow bridge connecting my young son's (secretly evil) heart with mine. Yesterday when I peeked into the bathroom, I expected to find him taking a bath only to discover that he had found something better to do. He was sopping wet and wearing enormous scuba goggles, huddled over the hot air vent with a towel ballooning around him: He was pretending to be a skydiver barreling toward earth. No words of explanation. He simply glanced up at me, wind flapping his hair, and grinned.

We have days that shimmer. We feel lit up by the shocking joy of connection and love. These are moments in each day when we might look at each other and say:

Whatever you are, I am.

Wherever you are, you can't drag me away.

We are the wild things that children's book author Maurice Sendak understood so well. At the thought of our separation, we gnash our terrible teeth and roar: *I'll eat you up—I love you so!*

We feel this way, ferocious in our love, because we know. We know how fleeting these moments can be. Some days are filled with fireworks, yes, but most are not.

We are living in difficult times, and we can see it all over our calendars. There's an appointment for a teenager's anxiety disorder or a visit to the nursing home. The mail is full of paperwork about the divorce, medical bills, school debt, or overdue credit cards. It would be embarrassing if someone else knew how much of our time gets sucked into arguments with our partner, our family, or the friend who's breaking our heart.

We want to be climbing metaphorical mountains, but who would do the dishes? Our problems feel unsolvable as they continue to go on and on and on. Sometimes loneliness or depression or health complications make life so small for so long that making plans at all feels ridiculous. Maybe a choice about school or a relationship, retirement or family drama, continues to keep our heads spinning. Our minds churn and our hearts lurch at the thought of what crisis we must confront next.

Or perhaps we feel the dullness of a set of obligations that makes each day a tight routine. Mondays are this. Tuesdays are that. There is little room for surprise or joy because flexibility is a thing of the past. Other people are taking vacations or having long dinners with friends, and we can almost taste the bitterness when we hear about it. I clearly remember a moment when the burden of my daily, weekly, monthly routine of cancer was so great that I briefly lost my mind when I saw two women sitting in front of a restaurant on a warm, spring day eating elaborate salads. And I yelled, "WHO HAS TIME FOR SALADS?!" I don't remember if those poor women heard me, but I could hear in my own voice that the question felt shockingly existential. Truly, who has time for salads when time is flat and hard?

Contrary to most of the advice of the self-help and wellness industry, our days are not simply a reflection of our choices. We are not a tally sheet of all our *yes* and *no* decisions. We like to imagine that we are built out of every small choice we made.

In fact, American culture (I say this lovingly, as a Canadian) makes it difficult to say otherwise. This is a country that heartily celebrates stories of self-made people whose every act of determination seems to bring them closer to greatness. And who wouldn't be inspired by the courage of seeing someone try and act and change?

But if we find ourselves caught up in a cultural framework that only prioritizes agency (our ability to act), this will make it hard to accept something that, deep down, we also know to be true: that most of what defines our lives happens *to* us.

The most fundamental aspects of our lives might have been different. To imagine it, we might pause and think of the major turning points in our own biographies. The stability of families we were born into. The safety (or danger) of neighborhoods we grew up in. The health (or disease) of our bodies and the opportunities that came our way, or didn't. The partner who left or stayed or never arrived in the first place. The love (or neglect) of our parents and children. The communities and churches who formed or malformed us. The babies we had, the ones we wished for, and the ones gone too soon. Our lives are less like a solid building standing on a perfectly poured foundation and more like a too-tall tower teetering like a game of Jenga. (In which case, contrary to what the Jenga advertisement jingle tells you, do not take a block from the bottom and put it on top. It's terrible advice. It's structurally unsound.)

We need a language of acknowledgment for the lives we *have,* not simply the lives we wish for. We need a spiritual account of time that is rich enough to name the breadth of our experience. Good. Bad. Difficult. Sublime. Mundane.

I started turning to the language of blessing when I realized that I needed bigger categories to describe my own surreal experiences. When I was thirty-five, I was diagnosed with Stage IV colon cancer. For the first few years, life was a crisis, a series of difficult, often life-or-death decisions that kept me and everyone who loved me in a state of perpetual fragility. As much as I am loath to say I "learned lessons"—I hate how suffering people are forced to say this—I did learn a great deal about my faith. I came to understand more about the beauty of a God who accompanies you to the very edge. My prayers changed from relatively elaborate confessions of faith (I am a professor in a divinity school, after all) into simple, raw hopes: *God, save me, save me, save me. And, God, if you don't, love me through.*

But then what was supposed to be a crisis turned into days and weeks, and I was not simply hurtling through the air. I needed to learn the language of the God who appears occasionally on a Tuesday, seems absent the rest of the week, but who has something to teach me when I'm actually *pretty* busy running errands, thank you. I needed God to be a part of my mountaintop and valley moments, but whose love was recognizable to me the rest of the time too.

There is a beautiful and instructive language that we can use for naming that strange mix of awful and divine experiences in our lives. And I've been hilariously late in using it, mostly because I thought I knew it already. It's the language of blessing. (P.S. When I was in my twenties, I wrote an entire history of the idea that God wants to give us health, wealth, and happiness and I called it *Blessed*. So yes. Perhaps a new understanding of blessing was a long time coming for me?)

American society is not a culture of blessing; it's a culture of *#blessed*. (If you want a brief education in the pervasiveness of this phenomenon, search for #blessed on social media and come right back once you stuff your cyeballs back into their sockets. It is . . . a lot of information.) Got that beach body by summer? #blessed. Trip to Maui on the calendar? #blessed. Is your family delightfully conflict-free and each child a scholarship recipient? Congratulations. You are #blessed and have thereby won social media.

From license plates to T-shirts to the entire line of home goods available to you at your nearest big-box store, #blessed has become one of the most common cultural clichés. Our society has taken a very precious truth about gratitude—that sometimes we feel so incredibly fortunate that we want to yell at the top of our lungs that *God is good*—and made ourselves the proof instead. We seem to be saying: *Aren't we actually pretty good too? Didn't we happen to put ourselves at the right place at the right time doing the right things, to be so lucky?*

But a blessing is more than a flush of gratitude for life's great gifts. Or a spiritual language for triumph. According to Old Testament scholar Stephen Chapman, the language of blessing is much wider and deeper.* And it is woven throughout scripture and the Christian tradition in a way that is far richer than I had previously understood.

What is a blessing? Chapman begins by explaining that, in its most basic form, a blessing is a particular kind of spiritual act of speaking. (The term for blessing pops up in both Greek and Latin to mean "to speak well.") And most often, blessings are pleasing to the ear. They are a form of poetry that calls on God and stirs up the hearts of its listeners.

Blessings are useful for all kinds of moments. We can bless each other as the joy of a greeting (Genesis 47:7). We can bless the food and water and sustenance of our

* Stephen B. Chapman, "Psalm 115 and the Logic of Blessing," *Horizons in Biblical Theology* 44 (2022): 47–63.

most basic needs (Exodus 23:25). But blessings are not simply expressions of thankfulness or affirmations of what God has done. We don't have to simply say that we are blessed for what we have already received. Or just repeat that God is good. Praise is good for our souls, but praise isn't identical to blessing. And prayer is good for our souls, but prayer isn't identical to blessing either.

The act of blessing is the strange and vital work of noticing what is true about God and ourselves. And sometimes those truths are awful. Like, *blessed are those who mourn*. I mean, scripturally it's true. Jesus said it. But does any of that feel true when our worlds are ripped to pieces? No. Or, *blessed are the poor*. Again, it doesn't feel true at all. But in the act of blessing the world as it is and as it should be, we are starting to reassemble what we know. Maybe, God, you are here in the midst of this grief. Maybe, God, you can provide for this specific problem or be discoverable when I'm buttering this toast.

For that reason, Dr. Chapman calls the act of blessing a kind of spiritual "placement." This goes here. That goes there. We are beginning to fit this moment into the larger order of things, the divine story of God's work and purposes. I find that language of placement and re-placement to be incredibly satisfying. Blessings put our spiritual house in order, even when our circumstances are entirely out of order.

When I bless the actual days I am living, I suddenly find I have a great deal more to say that is honest. I am mourning. I am bored. I am exhausted. I am apathetic. I discover that I am freed from the need to declare everything #blessed. Good or bad, I don't have to wait to say something spiritually true. I can simply bless it all instead.

How to Use This Book

Now feels like the right time to confess that I find spiritual habits to be very difficult. I rarely do the same thing more than two days in a row. So please hear in this a freedom to use this book as something you return to without feeling any guilt that you didn't read every entry one by one. In fact, Jessica and I imagined that you, our favorite reader, would look at the table of contents and pick out what you need that day.

We have ordered the blessings by the kinds of lives you might be experiencing: ordinary, tired, lovely, grief-stricken, overwhelming, painful, garbage, needing something for others, and, finally, beautiful but limited. We hope that somewhere in the mix of good and bad, joy and sorrow, you can find your place in God's presence.

We also wanted to make a plan for those of you who might be using this book during Advent or Lent, or both. You can find guides for those experiences at the start of "Bless This *Holy* Life" on page 196.

Whether you are a pastor who blesses your congregation or a chaplain who prays at hospital bedsides, whether this book is tucked in your dashboard to pull out in the carpool line or something you keep on the coffee table for a quiet moment, we want it to be a kind companion. Over the years of serving our digital community and listeners of our podcast, *Everything Happens,* we have had the privilege of learning a lot from people about what we need from God and from others. First and foremost, we need honesty. We need a place to reckon with the unresolved pain of being a human being in a world that prefers a slick solution. Second, we need courage. We need to be reminded that we are promised God's actual presence and the tangible love of spiritual community. And, lastly, we need hope. We need to be returned to the story of God saving the world, largely because our own efforts in the meantime will be a failure. But with honesty, courage, and hope, we will have a lot more love to sustain the lives we actually have.

So may the words that follow be a little shelter for you, dear reader. May these blessings meet you today, giving enough hope or courage or rest for this moment. And may they offer you words if you can't find your own, and some encouragement as you do what you always do: bless others.

bless this
ordinary
life

01
for this ordinary day

Lord, here I am.

How strange it is,
that some days feel like hurricanes
and others like glassy seas
and others like nothing much at all.

Today is a cosmic shrug.

My day planner says,
rather conveniently,
that I will not need you,
cry for you, reach for you.

Ordinarily, I might not think of you at all.

Except, if you don't mind,
let me notice you.

Show up in the small necessities
and everyday graces.

God, be bread.
Be water.
Be laundry.

Be the coffee cup in my hands
and the reason to calm down in traffic.

Be the gentler tone in my insistence today
that people pick up after themselves for once.

Be the reason I feel loved
when I catch my own reflection
or feel my own self-loathing
fluttering in my stomach.

Calm my mind,
lift my spirit,
make this dumb, ordinary day
my prayer of thanks.

"Earth is so thick with
divine possibility
that it is a wonder we
can walk anywhere
without cracking our
shins on altars."

—Barbara Brown Taylor,
An Altar in the World

02

for feeling it *all*

Blessed are you who feel things *big*.
You who might feel embarrassment because of
how overwhelming things can be.

Blessed are you who need reminders that those
emotions are not bad or good.
They are just . . . information.
> *You feel angry because this is unjust.*
> *You feel sad because this is awful.*
> *You feel tired because this is exhausting.*

Your emotions are not wrong or bad
or lying to you or telling the full truth.
They are giving you a bit of data
that you shouldn't ignore.
We love, and lose, and fall, and get back up,
and fail, and try again.

Your humanity is not an affront.
We are reminding ourselves that
this is who we are, how we're made:
to feel the pain, the grief, the stress,
the risk, the fear, the heartbreak.

So, you beautiful creature,
here is your permission slip to feel it all.
To feel the joy and delight and excitement.
And the sorrow and fear and despair.

All the yellows and pinks, and violets and grays.

Because you are the whole damn sky.

for when you just need to put one foot in front of the other

Oh God,
the thought of trying for a new and improved me
makes me tired.
I am barely getting anywhere,
so draw me closer to a different vision,
one that sees that I don't need perfection—

I need love.

Free me from the expectation
that life should always be better.
From the everyday stressors—
the bills, the pressure, the dependents,
the existential fears about the future
and the worries of right now.

I am threadbare.

Blessed are we, remembering
that the world is not ours to shoulder alone.
Help us put one foot in front of the other
as best we can.

Oh God, today,
give us enough to go on,
give us hope to see a future,
give us joy to see a present
lit up by your love.

P.S. And give me only enough humility
to be reminded that I look terrible in hats.
I mean, truly, unphotographable.

for when you're scared your kids are not getting the school experience they need

God, you know how often
this fear rises
like bile in my throat.
I look at my kid
—that miracle, that surprise—
and realize I have no idea what to do.

This child of mine has needs
I cannot fill.
Am I failing, God?
Couldn't I be more, somehow?
This helplessness feels like defeat.

Wait. I forgot again.
You never asked me to be unlimited.

God, surround this family.
Give us a safe and strong
and beautiful year.

We have seen our kids suffer too long
from the strangeness of growing up
    now, like this,
with worries that they can't even
    articulate,
from things they don't even realize are
    there.

"And he took the children in his arms,
placed his hands on them
and blessed them."
—Mark 10:16, NIV

God, what a thought:
that you can take our kids
and hold them, bless them.
Give them a school experience
   that works,
that feeds their growing minds,
and sustains their (ridiculous,
   wonderful) spirits.

And blessed are we, their parents,
who reach for you
(for we are your children too)
and ask to be blessed too.

In the meantime,
help us keep learning,
and creatively support them,

their schools, and their teachers,
that our kids might
grow up beautifully,
full of grace and courage.

P.S. And if your kid
(big or small) doesn't mind,
take them in your arms.
In this moment, love is enough.
For both of you.

for what makes us *us*

"Turn around and believe that the good news that we are loved is better than we ever dared hope, and that to believe in that good news, to live out of it and toward it, to be in love with that good news, is of all glad things in this world the gladdest thing of all."

—Frederick Buechner, *The Clown in the Belfry: Writings on Faith and Fiction*

Blessed are you, the strange duck.
You with the very intense hobbies.
Or the collection of movies or mugs or sneakers.
You with the hometown or home team
that makes you very, very proud.

Not everyone will get it,
but these are the things that bring you delight,
that let you swim around in the weeds
of who you are.

Blessed are you who have found your people.

The ones who understand. *Or who seek to.*

The ones who are up for the adventure or the hunt or the search.

Blessed are the details of your life. The specificities that make you, *you.*

The things you notice and the places you want to visit.

The eBay search you return to time and again.

The convention that's been on your calendar for months.

No matter how quirky or random or obscure.

You, my dear, in all your intricacies . . . *are a marvel.*

for when you are looking for love (and it's complicated)

This heart. I don't always know it well,
but it beats and breaks.
These must be the terrible clues
to how I am made:
    in love and for love.

Blessed am I, the beloved,
granting myself permission
to see afresh what I love, and who I love,
and how it is that I bring into the world
the singular and necessary and irreplaceable gift
that is me.

Unreservedly.
Embarrassingly.
In the strange confines
of this imperfect day,
let us decide that this thrumming pulse,
in its beauty and its breaking,
will finally be the proof that
in the giving of love,
we receive.

07

for feeling like your work matters

Blessed are we who remember that we are
not our job titles or paychecks or 401(k)s,
but we are being called, *whether we like it or not*,
to something greater than ourselves.

God, what is your call on my life?
I am listening.

Blessed are you who wonder
if you'll ever find your vocation.
You who desire to be part of the solution
to the world's pain.
May God nudge you in exactly the right direction,
where your gifts meet great need.

Blessed are you if you have stepped away
from a job due to retirement
or a diagnosis or a life change.
Life is different, but your purpose remains.

Blessed are you when you wonder
if your calling will cost too much—
you who do the good, hard work of serving others.
The way you pour out may often go unnoticed.
But today, may you feel fresh wind in your sails
because this is more than a job:
this is a call.

In our inbox, bless us.
In our conference calls, bless us.
When we clean and build,
punch in and punch out,
grant us meaning.

Give us people to serve,
customers to love,
good work to do.

And pour back into us more than we pour out.
After all, we're only human.

"We are called to be a
particular point of glory.
Fully alive. Dwelling
fully in the call of God.
The whole person is
then a space for God to
resound."

—Kirsten Pinto Gfroerer,
Anchorhold

for small steps
when you feel overwhelmed

Life has unraveled. All my plans, wrecked. My hopes, impractical.
And it seems daunting to imagine what comes next.

The bills that need paying.
The texts that need responding to.
The loneliness that seeps in every night.

Blessed are you who need reminding that,
yes, a lot of things aren't fixable or even tackle-able right now,
but there's something you might try instead.
Taking that tiny step that might make today a smidgen lighter.
　　　Maybe not easier or necessarily better—but lighter.

Being extra generous to a stranger or hopping in bed a little earlier.
Asking a friend to grab coffee or listening for the birds
instead of doom-scrolling Twitter.
Setting down our to-do lists and picking up a paintbrush
for no reason at all except joy.

May we be people who anchor ourselves to the now.
Not allowing our minds to skip to the what-ifs
or the what-will-happen-whens.

Blessed are you trying to put aside the "everything is possible" mentality.
You who know that sheer effort will not put these pieces back together.
You who have taken yourself off the hook for perfection,
and discover rest in "good enough" instead.

One small step,
one deep breath,
at a time.

**"Tomorrow will worry about itself.
Each day has enough trouble of its own."**
—Matthew 6:34, NIV

09

for
stretching
your heart

God, my life has too many things.
Awful. Lovely. Full. Shockingly incomplete.

Will you help me learn to live with a greater
    capacity for this?
Living in the tension between a life that has
    worked out . . .
and one that has gone to hell in every handbasket.

Let today be a divine exercise of *yes . . . and.*

Yes, I have so much to be thankful for,
and this hasn't turned out like I thought it would.
Yes, I feel moments of joy,
and I have lost more than I could live without.
Yes, I want to make the most of today,
and my body keeps breaking.
Yes, I am hopeful, *and* this is daunting.
Yes, I am trying to be brave, *and* I feel so afraid.

So bless me,
trying to live in between those two words:
yes . . . and.

May I understand this is where
the real work of life is found.
Where it takes courage to live.
Where grief can strip me to the studs
and love can remake me once again.
Where my heart can be both broken
and keep on beating.
Never sorry to have broken at all.

Yes . . . and.

Make me capable of great joy,
great love,
great risk,
even fear,
as you expand my heart
with this *yes . . . and* today.

10

for a
peaceful
day
or night

Oh peace, you are the mountain
we glimpse from afar,
the height and depth of our needs.

We chart our way to you by starlight
through paths overgrown
with wrongs we ourselves have seeded,
then left to grow unchecked.

It's a long way we travel, but a good one,
making things right as ever we can.

Light the way, God.
Bring us to that place of rest.
Rest from the world outside,
and the one inside.
Rest from our prickling fears
and obsessive thoughts:

What if this never changes?
What if this goes on forever?
What if I try and I fail?
What if I don't and never know?

Bring us peace, God,
enough for this moment.
Enough to quiet the questions with no answers.
And, while you're at it,
pencil us in for tomorrow, too.

bless this
tired life

for this tired day

11

God, sometimes I worry
this tiredness, this deep weariness,
is a sign of my failure.

Couldn't I *do* more?
Shouldn't I *be* more?

My library is full of books
reminding me to maximize my mornings,
empty my inbox, and optimize my routines.

But then you sneak in a reminder—
I am made delicate.

I grow tired after short bursts of effort,
and my body short-circuits.
I imagine worlds to conquer,
people to care for,
junk drawers to empty,
but I am spent
long before everything is finished.

God, erase my humiliation
about being stubbornly finite.
Remind me again
how all these limitations
can still be called *blessed*.

Blessed are my bleary eyes
and long naps.
Blessed are my scattered thoughts
and unfinished checklists.

May my mortality feel as beloved
as my efforts.
Because, in all things,
I long to be yours.

for when
you can't sleep

Oh God, again I lie here.
Awake.
Too tired, too restless, for sleep to come.
How will I ever get through tomorrow?
Oh God, bring peace to my mind and body,
and blanket me in the heaviness of slumber.

Blessed are we, still awake in night's loud darkness, who say:
Oh God, help me. You know the state I'm in.
My mind is a runaway train,
and my body, its captive.
You know all that troubles me.

Take hold of me.
Steady the racing of my heart.
Breathe fresh comfort through the whole of my being.
Wrap me in the secure knowledge of your love.
Remind me that tomorrow's worries can wait
because tonight has enough of its own.

Blessed are we who wait in the silence,
who remember that darkness is not dark to you,
who pray, oh God:
receive me,
gather me,
strengthen me,
sustain me,
and free me to tell you everything.

Blessed are we who listen in the quiet,
for you to breathe life
into all that is spent and gone,
filling mind and soul and body with hope,
and the beauty of your peace that passes all
    understanding,
gentle as the dawn.

Welcome one sweet thought.
Follow it . . . until it grows into genuine gratitude.

Rest there.

"Now guide me waking
and guard me sleeping;
that awake I may watch
with Your eyes, and
asleep, I may rest in
peace."
—The Compline, *The Book
of Common Prayer*

"Return to your rest,
my soul, for the Lord
has been good to you."
—Psalm 116:7, NIV

13

for truth-telling— however bitter or sweet

†

Blessed are you, resisting the urge to reframe.
You who are sick and tired of silver linings.

Blessed are you who risk sincerity,
especially when the world around you
craves a bright side.
You who speak honestly about
what is right in front of you:

> *This is hard.*
> *Things might not get better.*
> *This really has gone horribly.*
> *There may not be a different way.*

Blessed are you in your gratitude and your pain,
    your pleasures and your limitations.

Blessed are you, the truth-teller.
And what a miracle it is when
your candor finds a chorus that echoes back:
"Same."
The friend who will hear it.
The parent who will stomach it.
The partner who doesn't roll their eyes.

They hear you, and it feels like a revelation.
Every. Time.

May you feel your truths answered
by this language of love,
 changing where you can and
 confirming where you can't.

But loved, loved, loved all the same.

14

for when you're running on fumes

Sometimes I am paper
thinning at every touch.

Responsibilities and duties and errands
are wearing me down.
There is not enough time or energy
or finances or imagination.

I hardly recognize myself.

I can't keep going, but I can't rest.
God, can you help me slow down?

I just need a little shelter and a long breath.

Give me space to curl up for a while.
Hold me until I can feel my shoulders drop,
and I am freed from what can't happen right now.

Let me think only about what is gentle and lovely,
what is bountiful and unencumbered
on this too-heavy day.

Let me be amazed by nature and gaze in wonder.
At the sky. The velvet of petals,
and the precision of fronds.
The ridiculous owl with its stark yellow stare
and tweedy feathers.

God, scoop me up into life as it is.
Stop me from running ahead,
so I can be here,
in this space,
for the moment.
And breathe.

Amen.

for when the stress
is getting ridiculous

Oh God, worry has taken up residence
like an ungrateful guest.
She fusses and nitpicks and will not shut up.

God, bring ease to my mind,
and peace to my body.

God, have mercy.
Christ, have mercy.
Spirit, have mercy.

Oh God, you know what today is for,
you see my limited capacity—
the edges of my reach.

Use the fact that I am wildly forgetful
to help me set this all aside.

Blessed are we who live breath-to-breath,
when the nothing we can do
folds into stillness
and settles like a quiet pond.

Blessed are we when any tiny movement
becomes hope
and any gesture
looks a lot like love.

**"He makes me lie down
in green pastures.
He leads me beside
still waters.
He restores my soul."**
—Psalm 23:2–3, ESV

Take a moment.
Take the whole thing and nothing else.

Amen.

16

for when you're too tired to cry

Oh God, I am overwhelmed,
　　and somehow too tired to cry.

Oh God, I need to hear you say my name.

Oh my Creator,
speak me back into being.
Show me the bonds of love
　　that formed me in the womb,
　　that hold me still, now.

Let them be as iron
that enters my soul.

Blessed are we who see
that this present darkness
is not all there is.

Blessed are we who say:

I am known.

I am loved.

I can love again.

Even . . . especially . . . in this.

God, have mercy.

Christ, have mercy.

Spirit, have mercy.

Amen.

**"I have loved you
with an everlasting love."**
—Jeremiah 31:3, NIV

for when you feel stretched too thin

I am stretched so thin that
every task looms large.

At first, I thought I was still falling
but no, I've hit bottom.
I have no more to give,
yet so much more to do.

My resolve has dwindled
and my hope is chased away
by every anxious thought:
    Will this ever let up?
    Will I ever get a break?
    Will there ever be enough?

**"Those who trust in the Lord
will find new strength."**
—Isaiah 40:31, NLT

Oh God, show me again
how this works—
    how you bring dry bones to life.

God, have mercy.
Christ, have mercy.
Spirit, have mercy.

Blessed are we, the weary
and weak and sore,
with only the merest ember
left burning
but who still whisper,
with all the voice we can muster:

Breathe on me, oh God,
breathe life into my tired body,
my heavy limbs,

bring light to the dark corners
of my mind,
breathe comfort into my sad heart.

Enkindle my awareness
of who I was made to be
and of what is mine to do.

Blessed are we who turn our gaze
to seek the one whose eyes meet ours,
the one who knows us,
the one whose nail-pierced hands formed ours.
Like newborns whose bleary sight
focuses to find adoring eyes beaming down,
delighting and filling, mirroring and multiplying.

Blessed are we who discover
we are loved and held
in arms that are strong enough
to hold that which we cannot.

**"Come to me, all of you
who are weary
and carry heavy burdens,
and I will give you rest."**
—Matthew 11:28, NLT

18

for when you just can't find any peace

God, I am troubled in spirit
and there doesn't seem to be an end to it.
Show me the way toward peace.

Thank you for the freedom that comes
when I begin to admit
how powerless I feel, how small,
amid the mountains of trouble.

God, in this dark valley,
let your light reach me.
Let your Spirit comfort me.
Help me understand how my body
and mind and heart
can be at rest even here.

Jesus said,

"I have told you these things,
so that in me you may have peace.
In this world you will have trouble.
But take heart! I have overcome the world."
—John 16:33, NIV

Creator of heaven and earth and these mountains,
who created even me,
shelter me, live in me, breathe in me here,
alongside all that is too vast to comprehend.
You will never leave me.
It's a fact.
It's your greatest promise.

Amen.

"I look up at the vast
size of the mountains—
from where will my help
come in times of
trouble?"
—Psalm 121:1, The Voice

19

for when you need a little hope

✝

Oh God, these feel like darkening days,
with little hope to be found.
We cry out: Where are you, God?
And where are your people,
the sensible ones who fight for good?
Why does the bad always seem to
squeeze out all that is good?

Oh God, help us in our exhaustion
and in our desperation.
When we're tempted to throw our hands up
   in surrender,
anchor us in hope.

Blessed are we with eyes open to see reality:
the sickness and loneliness,
the injustice of racial oppression,
the unimpeded greed and misuse of power,
violence, intimidation,
and use of dominance for its own sake,
the mockery of truth, and disdain for weakness,
and worse—
      the seeming powerlessness
      of anyone trying to stop it.

Blessed are we who are worn out from cynicism
that we feel we've earned.
We who are running on fumes,
without the promise of a destination.

God, seek us out, and find us,
and lead us to where hope lies,
where your peaceable kingdom will come
and your will be done
on earth as it is in heaven.

Hope is an anchor dropped into the future.
We feel you pulling us toward it
once again.

**"Let not your heart
be troubled;
you believe in God,
believe also in Me."**
—John 14:1, NKJV

for when you're hanging on by a thread

The coffee is probably cold
because it's been reheated in the microwave once already,
and long-forgotten mugs are scattered around the house.
The kids are fighting in the other room.
It's another day of not calling Mom (and someone *really should*).
The dishes are gathering in the sink while another *chirp* from the phone
is a reminder that there are people—
friends, colleagues, loved ones—out there, right now
waiting, texting, wanting, needing.
And someone has to decide what's for dinner tonight.
Again.

So, because it must be true
(how else can we be permitted to be mortal?),
blessed are we, who want to set it all down.

Blessed are we when we're hanging on by a thread
or are unraveling at the seams.
Blessed are we who wonder if there is enough in this tired moment
for beauty and meaning and connection.

Blessed is our surrender, giving up the illusion of perfection.
Blessed are we who feel compelled to reach for what is possible instead.

May we feel something like contentment,
a grand permission to be basic,
without a five-step plan to master this day.

May we string together a thought or two
between each ordinary, stressful moment,
to wonder if this ridiculous day—
this too-full, too-heavy day—
might be surprised, even wowed,
by the sudden reappearance
of sparks of joy.

You were there, once before,
before the coffee and dishes,
before the fighting and the cell phone notifications.
There to be found, once again.

bless this
lovely life

21

for this
lovely
day

God, this season has been such a slog
that it's hard to remember what it was like
to be surprised by wonder.
I no longer notice the little things
that used to stop me in my tracks.

    Like the bird's song.
    Or the redbud's blossom.
    Or the twinkling sky.
    Or the sound of his laugh.
    Or their crinkly-nose smile.

They have become white noise,
a blur of details in my daily grind.

Refresh me, oh God.
Remind me of the loveliness found in today.
Surprise me with the details I have lost
the eyes to see.

Blessed are we, awakening from the
boredom of routine,
desiring to drink in from the beauty
around us once again,
full of the love you have given us,
the joy that is hidden among
the reeds of the ordinary.

Blessed are we who desire to feel our hearts soar
with the glory set in the heavens,
the moon and the stars,
with awe at the people right in front of us,
with the beauty of the lily in its elegant purity,
and the mystery and power of the tiniest seed,
bursting to life as it was always destined to do.

This world you made. It is irreducibly sublime.

Blessed are we who ask,
for hearts that are soft,
for eyes that are awake,
for ears that are open,
for hands to hold
the wonder that is here,
        now.

22

for a little boost in the morning

Today is new, oh God,
The light is gathering and spilling onto everything.
The sleeping and the sleepy.
The trees brushing the window.
Even the unwashed dishes know it's time.

What a gift.
Unopened.

Lord, you know the obstacle course ahead.
The intractability of most of my problems.
The irritations I will need to smile through.
The forgetfulness that will undo my best efforts.
And the fights I will need to pick because
someone really should.

But bring me back to this moment, God.
The gratitude that rises up within me
lifts my eyes and settles my soul.
Resurrection has happened again today—
you made the sun rise,
and brought love to the world already,
in the shape of a cross.

The hardest work is already done.
The work that remains is simply more of it:
more love, more trust,
more faith in the unseen pleasure you take
just gazing at us, sitting here.
We look ahead at a day that we can't control
but will be, somehow, already yours.

for when you need permission to change

Blessed are you, dear one,
when the world around you has changed.
Everything is different now:
> Your body, your age, your relationships,
> your job, your faith.
> The things that once brought you joy.
> The people you loved and trusted
> and relied on.
> The way you exist in the world.

Things have changed.
And it would be silly to imagine
you haven't been altered along with them.
You are not who you once were.

Bless that old self.
They did such a great job with what they knew.

They made you who you were
　　—all the mistakes and heartbreak
　　and naivety and courage.

And blessed are you who you are now.
You who aren't pretending things are the same.
You who continue to grow and stretch
and show up to your life as it really is—
　　wholehearted, vulnerable,
　　maybe a tiny bit afraid.

Blessed are you the changed.

24

for waking up to life again

Blessed are we, beginning to feel some release
from the crippling fear we've grown
far too accustomed to,
from the drawn-out season of anxious vigilance,
from the boredom and frustration of plans
     deferred.

Winter's long frost is over.
New ground has appeared,
and paths too we didn't know were there.

Blessed are we who need help waking up to
          the music, the movement,
          and the color of living,
          who need help trying on joy for a change.

The wonder of the daffodil,
the mystery and power of the tiniest seed,
cracked open and sprouting new life,
reaching, in its own time, toward the light.

Blooming.

Blessed are we who say, Wake me too, God.
Put me where beauty and love can reach me.
I'm ready for something new.

"Wonder is the heaviest
element on the periodic
table. Even a tiny fleck
of it stops time."

—Diane Ackerman,
   The Rarest of the Rare:
   Vanishing Animals,
   Timeless Worlds

for when you need a gentle day

**"To turn, turn,
'twill be our delight,
till by turning, turning,
we come 'round right."**
—Shaker hymn

God, I need a gentle day,
a respite from the strident voices
and the attention economy,
problems I can't solve.

I need a break.
God, shelter me awhile.

Blessed are we who come to you
just as we are,
asking to be gathered, hidden,
and held,
shielded for a time

from things too hard for us,
too heavy to hold for this long.

God, give us grace for one whole day
of gentle turning,
of turning away from worry
toward restful action,
of turning from the troubles
of yesterday or tomorrow.

Blessed are we,
when the unsolvable problem
comes to mind again,
to turn from it, just for now.
When checking the news
one more time seems a good idea,
to let the hands rest and
the computer screen go dark.

When the muscles in the body
speak their tight reminders,
to listen to them long enough
to give them release,
to gentle up the breathing
and lower the eyes,
to let ourselves be small again,
wrapped up, and lifted into your arms,
for long enough until
the stirrings of enoughness come—
enough energy to tend
just the little space
      that is within reach today.

"Blessed are we, looking to you,
for help to fix our minds
on gentler things,
on things that are both true
and honorable,
right and pure, lovely and admirable,
excellent and worthy of praise."
—Philippians 4:8 NLT (paraphrased)

for aging gracefully

Blessed are you who have reached
    a new age—
even if it doesn't seem to fit.
It may feel too big. Too reductive.
Too limiting.
It may be marked by a life
you barely recognize.

The kids who have all moved out
or settled somewhere far away.
The work that no longer
sets the daily hum.
The life partner who is gone
and friends you've outlived.
The body that doesn't allow
for the hobby you love anymore.
The monthly check that
doesn't provide the flexibility
you'd hoped for.

Wasn't I young just a second ago?
Will I ever recognize the person
    staring back in the mirror?
What's left to do that really counts?
How do I know if I am,
or ever was . . . enough?

Blessed are you who have lost so
    much.
You whose body hurts, and you
who aren't who you used to be.
You who no longer have
the identity markers that
once defined you so clearly.
You who attend more funerals
than weddings these days.
You who hold your new grandbabies
and have held your dying parents'
    hands.

God, give us eyes to notice the ways
life can still be beautiful
and rich and full
in the midst of so much
that has been lost.
Remind us that you
are not done with us yet.
For the God who spoke us into being
calls us even now.
Not to an ideal or a role,
but to a moment. This one.

In a world that equates
age with liability,
it's time for a reminder
that you are a gift.

You give advice.
You hold on to family recipes.

You remember that thing
that happened and, honestly,
we shouldn't have forgotten.
You think our kids are beautiful
and our bad partners
should be soundly dumped.
You kept the photo album.
You hold our stories.
Thank you.

Even when the world isn't paying
    attention,
may you get a glimmer of a reminder
that these little things add up
to something that is and always will be
beautiful.

27

for around the table

God, awaken us to the everyday miracle
of a simple meal.
Whether it is takeout that took a phone call,
or a recipe that took an entire afternoon,
or the cereal-for-dinner-again feeling
this meal creates,
bless it all.

So blessed are we, sharing a meal today.
May we recognize God's goodness
    in the thoughtful preparation,
    in the delivering,
    in the eating together,
        savoring something that tastes like love.

May our time around the table be a gift.

May we be present to one another,
engaging all our senses
as an act of thankful worship
for the nourishment that's before us
with the people we love. Or are trying to.

God, bless the hands that prepared this,
those with us now,
and the ones we wish were.
Bless us, oh God.
In all of our eating and cooking
and gathering and sharing,
     our jokes, talking with our mouths full,
     and elbows on the table,
     may we taste and see the love that multiplies.

Amen.

28
for friends who hold us up

God, you called me to love
but people are inherently risky.
Telling my story, being known, asking for help,
complaining again about
the thing I worry might sound cliché by now.
Shouldn't I be over it already?

But something is happening when I am known.
I am becoming stronger somehow.

I am reminded of the pillars I've seen
holding up cathedrals.
Flying buttresses, engineered to provide support
for a fragile wall,
allowing them to be built taller, more stunning,
more covered with ornaments
or filled with stained glass,
letting all the colorful light dance in.
The walls would collapse without them there,
but strengthened, they create something beautiful.

God, when I am no longer quite so tall and strong,
give me those who hold me up
and remind me of who I am and that I'm loved.

Yes, I'll get back up again today.
Yes, I'll get those kids cereal
and help my parents with an errand.
Yes, I'll go to work or come up with something
better to do with retirement hours.

I will try again.
I know I will,
because someone else's absurd faith in me
    is fortifying.

So, blessed are our flying buttresses.
For they hold us up
when everything seems ready to come apart,
allowing us to face today—
not because we're doing it alone—
but precisely because we aren't.

for learning to love yourself

When I don't feel worth loving,
God, help me remember
that you made me on purpose.

God, let me look through your eyes
to see the way you look at me
with pride and tenderness,
deep joy and love.

Every freckle put in place.
Every split end, numbered.
Every tear, bottled.
Every bad joke, laughed at.
All my limits and all my mistakes,
all my wild hopes and sometimes sour attitude,
All that makes me *me*
is a masterpiece
—*at least in your eyes.*

"Sometimes I feel lost,"
said the boy.
"Me too," said the mole,
"but we love you, and
love brings you home."

—Charlie Mackesy, *The Boy,*
the Mole, the Fox, and the
Horse

So, blessed am I, the one who sometimes feels unlovable,
the one who can't stop replaying that one horrible moment
over and over and over again,
never mind, it's been several years
and they definitely don't remember what I said.

Blessed am I as I shake off the embarrassment
of being human again today
in all my cringeworthy, foot-in-mouth moments,
in my old school photos, the crooked smiles
and the out-of-placeness I felt or still feel.

Blessed am I, as I try to feel at home in this skin,
remembering with more and more compassion
that this is me in all my unwieldy humanity.

Maybe humility is something like this:
    compassion for ourselves,
      because there are no preconditions to being loved.

30

for when it's been a great day

God, I want to bottle up the magic of this day,
and sip from it again and again.
I want to savor the taste of it, the beauty of it,
so I won't—can't—forget.

How is it, God, that such a day could
unfold so naturally,
and, at the same time, feel orchestrated for
   perfection?

It's as if it poured itself into my soul
and became the essential vitamin
I didn't know I was missing.

It appeared the way wild pansies do, suddenly,
their bright colors spreading
and growing effortlessly
in the hard ground, where nothing else will.

God, thank you
for this day that became for me
a gentle gift, and a heart at ease,
and hope blooming.

Blessed are we with open hands
receiving it gratefully,
carefully storing it away like a tea set,
ready to be poured out again
when friends stop by.

bless this grief-stricken life

31

for this grief-stricken day

†

God, we are heartbroken in the face of
so much evil, so much grief.
Comfort us in our sorrow.

Blessed are we who allow ourselves to feel it—
the impossibility
of what was possible a second ago—
  the light decision, the casual stroll,
  the easy exchange and ordinary duty,
  a decent choice or a banal one,
  the sweep of hours on a day that was like any
   other,
until it wasn't.

This is the place where nothing makes sense.
This is the place where tears flow in earnest now.

Blessed are we who allow our hearts to break,
for it will take some time
for brittle unreality to release us from its grip,
for the long and slow dissolve
until we fully see
what never should have been.

Blessed are we who ask you, God,
that grief find its way to move among us
and be felt together, that comfort may flow
in bonds of affection
unbroken by this fresh tragedy.
Though grief and tragedy and pain
try to convince us otherwise,
remind us that we are not alone.

God, have mercy.
Christ, have mercy.
Spirit, have mercy.
Amen.

"Behold, I cry,
'Violence!' but I
get no answer;
I shout for help, but
there is no justice."
—Job 19:7, NASB

for when the unthinkable happens

God, I am blindsided.
   What I thought was impossible
   . . . happened.

Is there language for
this disorientation, God?
   The unraveling of my sense
      of order.
   The way each familiar thing
   looks strange to me now.

Sometimes it seems that the gravity
that held the earth in place has been
   suspended.

It feels like a kind of unmooring.
   Fairness, undone.
   Justice, undone.
   Trust, undone.
   This life I loved, unmade.

I am trying to inch up to even the
   thought
that this is final. Unfixable. Over.

My mind is stumbling, God,
as if trying to rouse itself from a
   terrible dream.
When all I want to do is sleep.

My God, help me to know
   what to feel,
   what to do,
   what to pray,
   what to need,
   what to hope for,
      next.

Blessed are we who ask
      and wait,
      and ask again.

Blessed are we who let reality in
        though the body shudders.

God, you are the only story
about the world
        where truth and love make any
            sense.
        Remind me again.

**"My sheep listen to my voice;
I know them, and they follow me."**
—John 10:27, NIV

Show me the enormity
of the sky again,
        stretched above me.

And the comfortable weight
of the earth you made,
        holding me,
        resting just below my feet.

for the courage to try . . . and the wisdom to know when to stop

✝

**"God grant me the serenity to accept
the things I cannot change,
the courage to change the things I can,
and the wisdom to know the difference."**
—The Serenity Prayer

Blessed are you, *faced with the impossible*.
    You who do not take your eyes away
    from what threatens to swallow you whole.
    You who stare down reality,
    though your heart quickens.
    You for whom action comes swiftly,
        as you chart the next step
        or bulldoze a new path for yourself.
You know how to turn hope into action.
And bless you for it.

Blessed are you who, when you've come
to the end of what is possible,

> find the courage to live there too.
> Accepting the things that are unchangeable.
> And finding that beauty and meaning
> and love live there too.

You know what it means to have a life
held together by so many loves . . .
by so much to lose.

Blessed are we who are learning how to hope.

> And how to let go.
> When to act.
> And when to stop.

Holding together two irreconcilable truths:

> that our lives are so valuable
> precisely because we have so much to fear
> with this much to love.

34

for collective grief

✝

This world.
Impossible.
Unthinkable.
We are brought to our knees.

God, today, there is no true north.
And when I last checked,
the sun did not rise at all.
Today, the innocent still suffer,
buildings still fall,
families still grieve.
A world has ended without
any reasonable fanfare.

This is the way of tragedy,
how it breaks in and robs us while we sleep.

Help us to know what to feel,
what to do,
how to grieve—together.

Blessed are we
who try to see things clearly,
though the truth of it all feels
unimaginable.

Blessed are we
who ask and wait, and ask again,
for answers that may not come,
for hope that seems hard to find,
for comfort that is not easily offered.

Along the way
show us how to live
when we've lost the things
we cannot get back.

Remind us that you, oh God,
are our home and our refuge.
When life's unthinkable fragility
is too difficult to hold,
take my hands.

for the day of mourning

Love is in the particularities. Adapt this blessing with the appropriate name, pronouns, and details that describe the person you grieve.

Today we are drawn into mourning,
the complexity of love and loss
warms our hearts and chills our bones.

Just as the light of the sun
illuminates the lines of a spider's web,
invisible connections are revealed:
we are wrapped up in love.

Blessed are we who
acknowledge the way
our minds linger on the details.
We know exactly how
his mouth looked
when he laughed.
Or precisely what it meant when
she used *that tone.*

Blessed are you when you have
no reasonable plans
to make sense of a world
without them. How could we?
It would be easier to pour
the ocean into the kitchen sink—
this love is bottomless.

And blessed are we when we carry
this grief with no dignity.
Just some Kleenex and a look that
    says:
You don't know who died today.
How could you know
unless you felt the way time, today,
slowed until it meant nothing at all,
until I found him in my memories.

Oh God, you alone know
the whole of it,
        their sufferings,
        their joys,
        their hopes,
        their winding paths,
        every movement of their being.

Restore our souls,
even as you receive theirs.
Welcome them in with the kind of
    embrace we long to give.

Blessed is the time they were given
and the time you now have.
Whether in life or in death,
love is the greatest,
most stubborn truth.

for when disaster strikes

The world is not lost,
but sometimes it seems so.
With trees and homes uprooted—
and people's lives alongside them.
With wars raging on and violence unceasing.
With the utter randomness of disaster
and tragedies that don't seem to discriminate.
With hunger and homelessness and pandemics.

Blessed are we who cry out—
    How long, oh Lord?
The suffering we're witnessing is unbearable.
Come quickly.
Bring swift relief and sweet comfort to those in need.

Bless those who have lost everything.
Bless the helpers, the aid workers, the first responders.
Bless the leaders and peacemakers who are swift to act.
Bless the rescue workers, the shelterers, the neighbors.

And bless those of us who feel helpless in the face of such evil.
Give us clear eyes and sharp minds and courageous hearts
>   to know what little we might offer,
>   to ease pain where we are able,
>   to bear witness to what demands to be seen.

God, you know the need.
You are the beginning and the ending.
You have not left us alone.

God, have mercy. Christ, have mercy. Spirit, have mercy. Amen.

"And remember, I am with you always, to the end of the age."
—Matthew 28:20, NRSV

37

for when you've lost someone far too soon

"There are spaces of sorrow only God can touch."
—Sister Helen Prejean, *Dead Man Walking*

God, this. This is impossible.

This grief is too much to bear.

If there was a tight order
to the world that you made,
it's come unspooled
and no one will wind it up again.

God, I feel it coming,
that ache for the stories that will never be told.
And an anger rising
when I remember
what never should have been.

Worst of all—*God, could anything be worse?*—
it is so beautiful
the way this grief is a language of love.

I am lovesick with this much sorrow.

Teach me to speak this new mother tongue.
Show me how to memorize
so I can never forget
what they gave and what is gone,
and what we were owed
by a world robbed of their presence.

Hold me by the edges
for I am coming apart.
And nothing but love
will find me.

for when your parents are aging

"Even to your old age
I will be the same,
And even to your graying years
I will carry you!
I have done it, and I will bear you;
And I will carry you
and I will save you."
—Isaiah 46:4, NASB

The people I look up to
are growing older—
the ones I don't want to have to learn
    to live without.
I need their wisdom
and their courage now,
more than ever,
when time or illness or disease
is unrelenting.
Or they never became
the person they hoped to be.
And all I want to do is stop the clock.

Of course, I knew this would happen,
but find myself surprised
when I notice them
grayer, more delicate
than in my mind's eye.
I guess I thought they'd be around
    forever.
The adults in the room.
The ones who would always be
on my team,
or know the right answer
or what to do in an emergency.
But how our roles have changed.

Blessed are we with hearts
that desire to love well
        through the difficulties to come,
        the scary, the tedious, the sad,
amid the long, slow transition
that is weighted with anticipatory grief,

and yet is so full of promise for new
　　chances,
for new forgivenesses
and acknowledgments of past hurts,
for new graces that may slip into the
　　day.

How blessed are we in difficult
　　relationships,
we who seek to bind up the frayed
　　places,
to give comfort and receive it,
to reach out a hand, wordlessly,
and find peace.

Blessed are we who can even laugh
at the new strangeness of feeling
so human together,
and how the heat of old battles
(*what were they about again?*)
are almost cooling with time.

Blessed are we together
sharing one long look
that says: *What we have is
　　irreplaceable.*
It is a "we" that will remain,
no matter what.

**"He will wipe every tear from their
eyes. Death will be no more; mourning
and crying and pain will be no more,
for the first things have passed away."**
—Revelation 21:4, NRSV

39

for all the firsts without a loved one

Oh God, the calendar tells me a big day is coming
and this is the first one in this new reality.
I don't know how to get through it.

Show me what to do with
the memories, the traditions,
the pain, and the excruciating beauty
of all that was.

Blessed are we who come to you, oh God,
in the midst of grief and loss, fear and longing,
irritability and anger,
gratitude and sweet remembrance,
and so much exhaustion.

Blessed are we who say,
God, I don't know where home is
or who I am now.
Couldn't I just rest for a while?
I am too tired to feel everything there is to feel.
Too exhausted to face the truth.

Grant me solitude enough for solace,
and company enough for comfort,
people to be with who know how to slip quietly

under the burden of this grief
and shoulder it with me without much to say.

Blessed are we who ask you for permission
to do things the same way
or completely differently,
to wade through raw emotions
or ride on the surface of it all.
Give us wisdom and guidance
that transcends the strangeness,
making whatever little plans are possible.

Blessed are we who ask for a way forward
    during this time
to celebrate some small ritual of remembrance
that becomes a safe place
to store the love and the grief,
the anger and the ache of the knowledge
that there is no one who can take their place.
Not one.

"He heals the brokenhearted and binds up their wounds."
—Psalm 147:3, NIV

Blessed are we who ask you, God,
to take hold of the fear,
and us with it,
and lead us through.

for life after a loss

Blessed are you, who feel the wound of fresh loss.
> Or of a loss . . . no matter how fresh . . . that still makes your voice crack all
> > these years later.
> You who are stuck in the impossibility of it. Frozen in disbelief.
> *How can this be? It wasn't supposed to be this way.*

Blessed are you, fumbling around for easy answers or quick truths
> to try to make this go down easier.
> You who are dissatisfied with the shallow theology and trite platitudes.

Blessed are we, who, instead, demand a blessing.
> Because we have wrestled with God and are here.
> > Wounded. Broken. *Changed.*

Blessed are we,
>who keep parenting,
>who keep our marriages and friendships and jobs afloat,
>and who stock the pantry . . .

because . . . *what choice do we have*
>but to move forward with a life we didn't choose
>with a loss we thought we couldn't live without?

One small step. One small act of hope at a time.

bless this overwhelming life

for this overwhelming day

✝

"It is the narrowness
of the riverbanks,
after all, that gives
strength to the river."
—Rob Des Cotes

God, I am trying to juggle too much,
but I don't know what else to do.
Or who else will keep everything
in the air,
if not for me.

Blessed are we who say,
Jesus, I'm taking you at your word.
I am coming to you just as I am,
burnt out, craving rest,
but still tempted to keep going
like I always do,
propelled from one task to the next
as if the earth spins because I do.

But I know, deep down,
that this is unsustainable.

Blessed are we,
quietly closing the door,
willing to fold ourselves into
this present moment.

Slow me down, God.
Place your hand upon me
and steady the racing of my heart.
Take this weight from my shoulders,
and pry these to-dos from my fingers.
Deepen my breath and still my mind
so that I can remember whose hands
really do keep the stars hung in space.

**"Before the mountains were born
or you brought forth the whole world,
from everlasting to everlasting
you are God."**
—Psalm 90:2, NIV

I know by my body's limits
and the clock's relentless ticking
    that not everything has to be
      done,
    and not everything has to be
      done by me.

Blessed am I,
beginning to recognize that my edges
as well as my gifts can shape
the natural contours
of what is mine to hold,
and mine to do.

God will take care of all
that you can't, dear one.
And you, too.

42

for when you can't catch a break

†

"I will hide beneath the shadow of your wings until the danger passes by."
—Psalm 57:1, NLT

The sheer absurdity of these problems could almost make me laugh.

Just as one trouble fades, two more appear.
Like a game of endless Whac-A-Mole.
Unbeatable. Absurd.

In our desperation and flooded minds,
blessed are we when we cry out:
    God, help me,
       here,
       now.

Blessed are we who look for you, oh God.
    You who promise to comfort us
    in our troubles.
    and sing over us in the night.
    You who promise to strengthen our hearts.

Blessed are we, who hope . . . still . . .
> that some small good might yet be done.
> Yet at this moment may it be enough
> *just to be.*

May our eyes close, and soften into stillness.
> For God is awake.

God, have mercy.
Christ, have mercy.
Spirit, have mercy.
Amen.

"With unfailing love I have drawn you to myself."
—Jeremiah 31:3, NLT

for when you need a second to think it over

Blessed are you who don't have
all the right answers.
You who realize that "I don't know"
is the best response and posture for now.
You who lean in, unafraid to learn
and change and be wrong along the way.

Blessed are you,
      stretched and pressed and pulled
      by the uncertainty,
      deciding to not stay the same
      because *we are not who we were.*

We have been pulled into the unknown
without our permission.
But the challenge is the same:
reveal truth in love in the midst of seeming chaos.

Blessed are you who realize that
community can help see truth more fully
even if your chin has to be turned gently toward it.

Being fragile amid a world of hammers
takes courage
      to be wrong,
      to learn something new,
      to choose humility and kindness
      over being right.

May we be a people who don't have it all together
(and who are done posturing).
Curious, hopeful, courageous.

Amen.

44

for caregivers

Blessed are we
for whom the call to loving action is still strong,
whose every urge is to keep going, keep working,
and not to count the cost.

And yet blessed are we,
beginning to notice that we are
slowing down, inexplicably,
or just pausing, staring for no reason,
or starting something,
but then quickly turning to another demand.
We who realize that we are beginning
to lose the thread.

Blessed are we who say,
I really can't keep going like this,
at this pace, under this weight,
and the momentum is so strong.

God, come and be the hands that sit me down
and keep me there long enough
for me to really feel what I feel,
and know what I know.

Come and be the wisdom
to find that the community is broad enough,
kind enough, effective enough
to meet the needs that are here
—both mine and theirs.

Come and be the peace that frees me
to let my hands lie gently open awhile,
the grace to just receive.

Seek the rest you need,
and a little bit more.
And breathe.

45

for when you suffer alone

✝

I see you there, suffering alone,
with the illness or pain that lingers,
though friends do not
        —or cannot.

You, in isolation,
locked in or locked out.

You, the caregivers
struggling in the certainty
that there is not enough
        strength, time, or resources.

You who counsel others in their trauma,
but suffer deeply from your own.

You who are grieving losses, too many to name,
too complex or unbecoming to speak aloud.

Blessed are you, dear one,
searching for someone to understand,
to see your wounds and your hope for healing.
You are seen, as you walk this hard
and lonely road.

Blessed are you because your loneliness
speaks a deep truth:
you were never meant to do this alone.

God, comfort us, guide us,
that our hope for *more*—
a prayer which will be answered—
might be protected too.

for the gift of doubt

"My Lord God, I have no idea where I am going. I do not see the road ahead of me. I cannot know for certain where it will end, nor do I really know myself . . . But I believe that the desire to please you, does in fact please you."
—Thomas Merton, *Thoughts in Solitude*

I long for understanding,
but life is full of unanswered questions.

Oh God, reveal to me what I need to know now,
    and as for the rest . . .
      teach me how to live with so much uncertainty.

Blessed are we who come to you in the discomfort of our doubt,
    for we trust that our honest unknowing is a truer and better prayer
      than bootstrapping efforts at certainty.

Blessed are we, receiving the gift of doubt,
    for we trust that it is a doorway, freeing us to become
      all that we could not otherwise have known.

Blessed are we, remembering that you hold all things together.

You are the invisible scaffolding that supports us,
  the canopy of love that covers us in the present,
  the stable pillars, sunk deep into our past,
  and the sparrow that flies confidently toward the future
    bearing for us the peace we could never have attained for ourselves.

Blessed are we, settling into the truth that there are things that we can't know,
  settling into the humility that knows this one thing:
  that we are of the earth, while you bear up the universe.

**"Doubt is not a pleasant condition,
but certainty is absurd."**
—Voltaire, *Complete Works of Voltaire*

47

for when the road is long

---

†

"The Lord says: Stand at the
crossroads and look;
ask for the ancient paths, ask where
the good way is, and walk in it."
—Jeremiah 6:16, NIV

"Fear not, for I am with you;
be not dismayed, for I am your God;
I will strengthen you, I will help you."
—Isaiah 41:10, ESV

Sometimes when we feel lost,
floating outside of what we know,
who we wanted to be
and where we wanted to be,
it's tempting to feel small
and wonder, *Maybe*.
Maybe I should just
shut this down a bit.
Maybe no one needs to hear from me.
Maybe that's enough for now.

Oh God, I could not have imagined
that this road could be so long
and so hard, and so daunting.
Yet here I am, worn out—
body and soul.

I feel exposed, vulnerable,
outside of what should be normal.
Oh God, I don't know what to do

to make this lighter,
easier, or go by any faster.

Help.

Blessed are we, the downtrodden,
who must set aside
what we are carrying
and begin to feel
only the weight of our own being.
It is enough for now.
Let our shoulders sink
from around our ears,
our breath grow longer and deeper,
taking a minute to notice
the way our diaphragm rises and falls
without us telling it to.

Blessed are we who cannot go on . . .
not like this,
but stand and look and ask,

Which is the good way to walk in?
Is there an easier route?

Blessed are we who listen
for the voice that is both
thunder and softest rain.

Blessed are we,
at the point of utter stillness
that becomes an empty space
for that voice to echo and build
and resound
until it becomes a place to rest
and receive and be made whole.

And oh, how blessed are we
who are astonished
to find that God's strength begins
at the very point
when ours runs out.

for courage when you don't feel very brave

God, I have no idea what courage is
or how to muster it,
but I know I need it.
Fear is taking up too much space
and I have so little bandwidth left.
God, if courage is a gift, then please give it.
And if it is a thing for me to learn,
then show me how.

For blessed are the brave.
Those who perform big courageous
acts of sacrifice.
Those who move toward fear and danger
so the rest of us feel a little more safe.

May we also learn bravery
in small acts of great love.
We who grieve, even if we feel like
we are doing it all wrong.

We who have received the bad news and take the
    next right step toward what must be done.
We who sit in the shards of a life
that has come undone.
We who hold another's hands
on their hardest days.
We who serve and pour out and keep loving,
no matter the cost.
We who live still,
brave and scared at the same time.

Perhaps fear is not something to be vanquished,
but rather that strange friend who tells us
who we love, and what we can't live without.

So bless us, God.
In our fear. In our shaky hope.
Because brave looks like that too, sometimes.

**"For God has not given
us a spirit of fear,
but of power and of love
and of a sound mind."**
—2 Timothy 1:7, NKJV

for when you feel forgotten by God

✝

"The Lord bless you and keep you; the Lord make His face shine upon you, and be gracious to you; the Lord lift up His countenance upon you, and give you peace."
—Numbers 6:24–26, NKJV

I don't know how to say this
   any other way:

This is too much.
I am in a body that needs healing,
in relationships that need restoring,
in a whole world
that needs redeeming,
and I am in over my head.
And I feel jealous when others
seem to have it all together,

have lives that seem to be
working in their favor.
What about me, Lord?

God, please start it now:
the promised healing, restoration,
   redemption.
I can't wait much longer.

Blessed are we who pray
like a faith-filled child:
Help me feel better soon.

Heal me from the pain I suffer,
and let me see good days again.
Send relief through the
competent hands of professionals
whose training has prepared them,
and whose disposition propels them
to seek out the answers that can make
a difference for me and for others.

Restore the brokenness between me
and the people I struggle to love.
When caring for my actual neighbor
seems too big an ask.
When my family is frustrating
and colleagues difficult.
When my kids drive me nuts
or my partner is selfish.
When my friends let me down
and my mentors disappoint me.
When I feel alone, wishing I had
what others do.

Redeem the whole world
alongside me:
the old and the young,
the sorry and sad,
the angry, the vengeful, the snide,
the mindless, the innocent,
the misguided,
the cruel and powerful,
the weak and frail,
the prisoners and protesters,
the politicians and police,
the scientists and engineers,

the nurses and doctors,
the workers and unemployed,
all the sick, the hungry, poor,
and homeless,
the lonely and the dying,
every soul in all your creation.

Oh God, let your goodness prevail.

Blessed are we, the in-over-our-heads,
who do all that we can do:
lament honestly and pray continually,
and be truly glad for others
when their relief comes,
when their relationships are restored,
or when they experience
a measure of peace.
For we are not diminished
by their fortune.
But rather, emboldened to pray:
Me too, Lord!

Receive this blessing. It's for you.
Then pray it for someone else too.

50

for when it is too much to handle

**"How frail is humanity!
How short is life,
how full of trouble!"**
—Job 14:1, NLT

My body remembers the sleepless nights
and cold sweats and unrelenting stress.
Though the worst is through,
I don't know how to move on.
I'm wary to trust it is really over.
I don't know when I can stop being afraid.

God, show me how to process all this.

Blessed are we, when we decide
to make room for all of it,
the fear and the gratitude,
the complexity and the suffering.

Blessed are we who pour out to you
the whole of it—
unedited—all the terrible truths
and fears and what-ifs.

The gratitude for those beautiful hearts
in action who came willingly
into the strange and awkward space
that is my need.

Blessed are we, learning as humans together
that pain is inevitable,
nurses are wonderful, hospitals are loud,
people are brave.
And we grow and we hurt and we heal,
and then we do it all over again.

Feel everything. Invite your emotions to tea,
    and listen.
They might not stay long.

**"But even when I am
afraid, I keep on
trusting you."**
—Psalm 56:3, CEV

bless this
painful life

for this painful day
(and our bodies feel like the enemy)

Blessed are you on this pain-filled day.

When getting out of bed seems to be an award-worthy triumph.

When you can't remember what it feels like to not be so aware of your own body.

When you arrange your weeks around appointments or side effects.

Or when you stop telling the truth altogether—

    about how bad it hurts,

    how scared you are of your own mind,

    or the boring details of another non-diagnosis—

because you are afraid people have stopped caring.

You speak a language of suffering the world doesn't try to understand.

Blessed are you whose world has shrunk to a space so small

it's defined most by what is no longer possible.

You count, dear one.

And so does your pain.

It does not and did not disqualify you from belonging.

For the truth of it is, life is painful,

and what makes it so

is the terrible and the beautiful
living side by side.
Our loves. Our losses.
Our limits and hopes.
Our successes and failures.

Some would try to sell us the fiction
that there's an invincibility club,
and we really should join.
If only we could qualify.

But our God came to be cloaked
in our fragility,
in our humanity,
to know our pain from the inside out.

Oh suffering one, you will never, ever be left behind.
You belong. You are loved.
And you have never been forgotten.

Come join us, in the company of the broken.

for finding grace for others (and ourselves)

Blessed are we, the graced.
We who don't deserve it.
Whose failures haunt us.
>   The things we said.
>   The things we left unsaid.
The decisions and addictions and broken relationships
that have ripple effects we feel still today.
Somehow, we are the recipients of this mysterious gift.

Grace doesn't erase the pain or harm we've caused.
But grace, still.
For us, the redeemable.

And if we are . . . that means *they* are too.
Yes—even them:
>   The rude neighbor.
>   The estranged father.
>   The unforgiving ex.

The boss who screwed you over.
The doctor who messed up.
The selfish pastor.
The family member who did the unthinkable.

Despite what we all have done and left undone. We are graced.

Blessed are all of us who wrestle with unforgiveness and ungrace.
You who make amends.
You who reach for forgiveness.
You who say you're sorry even when sorry will never be enough.
You who find the bridge to forgive the wrong done to you.
Even when you cannot forget. Or can't go back.
Or they aren't *nearly* sorry enough.

Blessed are we who live here. In this mystery, this scandal, of grace.

53

for if you've had a painful childhood

Blessed are you who come with your sorrow,
allowing your pain to convey all its truth.
For here in the arms of Jesus
is where reality is a welcome guest.
Here is where grief is understood at its core,
where the dark shadow of betrayal
is seen from the inside.

Here, my dear, is where the work
of healing begins.

Blessed are you who mourn
as you meet yourself once again as that little child
who needed protection but did not receive it,
who deserved respect but was not afforded it.

The things that should have happened but didn't
and the things that happened but shouldn't.

The broken family systems and
normalized cruelties
that allowed your pain to continue
far beyond what it should have.

For you have come now to the God
who is alive to your past,
your present,
and your future,
who has already moved heaven and earth
to restore your dignity,
and return you to yourself.

P.S. Take a minute to remind your past self
that you are loved now, tomorrow, and forever.
And rest. You are safe. You are held. You are loved.

for when you've been hurt by the church

God, you saw me walk away.
I had to.

For what was supposed to have been a refuge,
a community of hope, purpose,
mutual encouragement,
distorted all I understand you to be.

Oh God, lead me to the heart of love,
so I might find the healing I need,
and protect the reverence I have for you.

For you do not consume, but rather feed.
You do not destroy, but build up.
You do not abandon your little ones,
but insist that they belong in your arms.

Enfolded here, I see you now,
the God who loves us to the end.
For though I walked away, you didn't.

You found me. And will lead me.
Let's now find the others.

55

for when hope seems lost

✝

Hope is only a half-remembered
   dream
behind a closed door.

All is lost.

God, this reality is a current so strong
I feel certain, at least for now,
that it will sweep us all away.

Could you bless this honesty
that feels like despair?

**"Weeping may endure for a night,
but joy comes in the morning."**

—Psalm 30:5, NKJV

Can we whisper that, somehow,
blessed are we,
with spirits starved for what is good?

Allow our eyes to see the small,
sealed space
where pain has isolated us.

We cry: God, help me.
I can't break out of this.
So please, break in.
Cut through the walls
of this hard prison,
and flood it with the light
of your presence.

Make prayer as natural as breathing
to release to you all that I know
and think and feel,
and inhale deeply
some of your goodness and strength.

Blessed are we when we realize
that suddenly, already,
you never leave. You insisted on
breathing life and hope and truth
into my lungs,

filling everything,
until the pain dissolves
and I am free to move in faith again.

Blessed are we who have
a glimmer of certainty
that in that dark expanse,
and as sure as day follows night,
hope returns.

P.S. Take a deep breath.
Let a yawn come, and another.
See what new thing begins.
All by itself.

for when this pain doesn't make sense

God, I'm fumbling around for answers, reasons, meaning.
I can't find any purpose in this pain.
> Why me?
> Why them?
> Why now?

I don't know when this is going to get better.
Or if I will ever feel relief.

God, make this pain matter . . . at least to you.
See me in my fragility.
Give me a reminder of your presence.
> Reach for me,
> for I am too weary to reach for you.

Blessed are we who need to be reminded
> that there are some things we can fix
> . . . and some things we can't.

Blessed are we who can say:
    My life isn't always getting *better*.

Right in the midst of the pain and fear and uncertainty,
may we hunt for beauty and meaning and truth . . . together.

Not to erase the pain or solve the pain
    (though surely *that would be nice*),
      but to remind us that beauty and sorrow coexist.
      And that doesn't mean we're broken or have been forgotten.

God is here, and we are never—*were never and will never be*—alone.
In our hope. In our disappointment. In our joy. In our pain.

God, have mercy. Christ, have mercy. Spirit, have mercy. Amen.

57

for when you're tired of broken systems

†

Oh God, I am done with broken systems
that break the very people
they are meant to serve.

Harness this anger!
Channel it into worthy action and show me
what is mine to fix and what boundaries to patrol
to keep goodness in and evil out.

Blessed are we who are appalled
that brute ignorance can so easily dominate
over decency, honesty, and integrity.

Blessed are we, who choose not to look away
from systems that dehumanize, deceive, defame,
    and distort.
We who recognize that thoughts and prayers
    are not enough.
We who stand with truth over expediency,
        principle over politics,
            community over competition.

Oh God, how blessed are we who cry out to you:
Empower us to see and name what is broken,
what is ours to restore.

Guide us to find coherent
and beautiful alternatives
that foster life, hope, and peace.
Help us to use our gifts with one another in unity.

Blessed are we who choose to live in anticipation,
our eyes scanning the horizon
for signs of your kingdom—
heaven come down—
            as we wait.

**"They have forsaken me,
the spring of living water,
and have dug their own cisterns,
broken cisterns that cannot hold water."**
—Jeremiah 2:13, NIV

58

for when your family disappoints you

God, I am angry and hurt and so incredibly sad.
The very people who were supposed to love me
and know me best
    have let me down.
I don't know if I'll be able to let this go
    or find a way forward.
    I am losing my sense of home.
And the reality of it all fills me with a kind of fear.
However big, however small,
this pain always feels . . . unforgivable.

I know they are only human (*really, I know*),
but their mistakes feel like they echo through me.
They strike a painful chord that rings on and on.
I feel convinced, all at once,
that I am not loved, not known, not safe.

I feel small, all over again.

**"Though my father and mother forsake me,
the Lord will receive me."**
—Psalm 27:10, NIV

So bless me, God, when tears prick at my eyes,
and I feel lost to myself.
Bring me home.
Remind me of the places you've brought me,
the person I've become,
when I feel your light and peace.
Forgive them for me when I can't
and send some grace for this moment,
to keep my heart from breaking
or my temper from rising
or any sentence from starting with
"YOU ALWAYS . . ."

You remember me when I am a stranger to myself,
and an outsider at my own address.

"Behold, I am making all things new."
—Revelation 21:5, ESV

for when your child is in pain

Oh God, my child is hurting
and I can't seem to make it better.
Please come and ease the suffering,
and show me if there is something I can do.

Blessed are we who open our palms to you,
oh God,
these useless hands that can do nothing.
Blessed are we,
released from the isolation of sorrow
and given grace to pray:

Oh God, this is your child too.
You know every cell in this one you have made,
every movement of heart and body,
every need before it becomes thought,
every anxiety that keeps them from sleep.

I lift to you this precious child whose
body, mind, and soul you knit together.

**"Out of the depths
I cry to you, Lord;
Lord, hear my voice.
Let your ears
be attentive
to my cry for mercy."**
—Psalm 130:1–2, NIV

Bring every cell, every system into order,
that there be soundness, wholeness, and healing.
Restore beauty and resilience and hope,
and let the good days outnumber the bad.

Bring to bear any outside influence or resource that could make a difference,
good friends and support systems and kind professionals,
and make it effective, selfless, swift, and strong.
Blessed are we who pray:
Create moment by moment
a bridge from suffering to relief,
from distress to comfort,
from loneliness to loving community,
from the depths to level ground,
and a life that can function, grow, bless, and be blessed.

Let your prayers come and go with each reminder.
That is what you can do.

bless this
garbage life

60

for this garbage day

**"Blessed are the poor in spirit,
for theirs is the kingdom of heaven."**
—Matthew 5:3, NIV

I can find no good in today,
and I don't want to try.
It feels like a lie to sugarcoat reality,
instead of naming what is.
When there is much to grieve,
too many losses and disappointments
    to name,
too many things going wrong,
when I'm better off
climbing back under the covers
and trying again tomorrow.

Blessed are we, the Debbie Downers
and Negative Neds,
who come to you just as we are,
with our loneliness and loss,
our scarcity and sorrow,
and say, *God, there is just not enough.*
    Not enough money to pay bills.

Not enough jobs or safety
for those who have them.
Not enough wisdom
    to find solutions.
Not enough strength or comfort
    or connection.
Not enough patience
    to deal with these people.
Things are hard today.

Perhaps it is too much to say,
"God, thank you for today."
Because today is already
topped up with
frustrations and bad attitudes
and unhope.

So instead, may there also
be a blessing for those of us who say,

"God, could you come meet me here
    on this garbage day?"
Give me a microscope to notice
the tiny, tiny graces.
        The smell before the rain.
        The softness of my pet's fur.
        The way my friend
        gives the best hugs.
        Or that my favorite show
        always cheers me up.

So when gratitude feels impossible,
may I learn to compress my attention
so narrow as to find the smallest
    hopes.
Not as a formula to quiet the wrongs,
but as a practice of finding
any crumbs of joy
now visible on the kitchen floor.

for when you are afraid

†

God, I am paralyzed by fear.
Afraid my past might creep back to haunt me.
Afraid of what might happen next.
Afraid of what might not.

For my loved ones, my kids, my friends,
my parents, my job, my nation, and my world . . .
afraid, afraid, afraid.

Blessed are we who admit:
    "God, I'm afraid."
Blessed are we who confess:
    "I don't know how to stop
    this spin cycle of worry."
You know our anxious minds.
You fill our restless hearts.
You promise us your presence—
    the quiet of your love.

God, quiet my fears. Hold me when I feel
there is no place to stand.

For now, may I inhale and exhale your presence.
      Inhale: *For our God*
      Exhale: *is closer than air.*

God, have mercy.
Christ, have mercy.
Spirit, have mercy.
Amen.

**"My heart has turned to wax;
it has melted within me."**
—Psalm 22:14, NIV

62

for when you are waiting

God, here I wait.
Where the air is still
and presses in upon all possibility,
here in this waiting room with all the others—
    waiting for a diagnosis or for test results,
    for them to make a decision
    or my heart to finally know,
    for that letter in the mail
    or the headline to break,
    for the loved one refusing to change,
    or the child to find happiness at last.

God, here we wait,
in a place where fear and anger
and frustration come so easily,
and the simplest decisions seem to take forever.
Where we're reminded once again
that so little is in our control.

God, come and help us.
We need something—someone—
to make a difference.
We long for good news.

    Not the anticipation of realized fear
    we know too well.

Bring that ridiculous miracle.

    The phone call or news.
    The decision or the resolution.

But if it doesn't, God, bless *this*.
The place where love becomes the air we breathe
even here, in the waiting room.

for when you can't love yourself

---

†

God, I don't love myself, so how can anyone else?

Blessed are we who say,
God, maybe I can borrow some of your mercy,
as I unfold to you the unloveliness within.

And maybe as I hand it all over,
I can borrow some of your gentleness and grace
to use for myself,
to help me absorb some of these
fleeting feelings of love,
so I can breathe freely in my own company.

There is a buried secret, there,
somewhere in my mind
that I am more than worthy,
somehow cherished
in embarrassing detail.

Then, fine, I accept.
Inhaling this love gives life to everything else.

**"Rejoice that you are
what you are;
for our Lord loves you
very dearly."**
—Abbé Henri de Tourville

for when you're feeling grouchy

✝

God,
complaining is completely underrated.
How else can I be honest?

Every frustration has me spinning.
And the sheer volume
and timing of each new problem
has me convinced this is a conspiracy.
Are they trying to ruin this for me?

I'm trying.
I'm honestly trying here.

God, come meet me here.
Chip away at my chippiness.
Calm my racing heart.
Loosen this feeling in my chest.

Blessed are we when we notice
that the day is trending

**"For I have the desire
to do what is right,
but not the ability to carry it out."**
—Romans 7:18, ESV

in the wrong direction.
No matter how hard we try,
the answers are not coming,
and even the questions
have all trailed away.

Blessed are we when we recognize
that it's time to just stop,
find a moment alone,
And breathe.

Blessed are we,
who notice something emerging,
a memory of truth revealed,
of mercy received,
a comfort, a word.

And how grateful are we
who take the first step,
and find it has its own springs.

for when you're not getting any better

†

I'm not nearly the person I thought I'd be.

And this life is not what I would have picked.

Blessed are we who say:
God, I have come to the end
of my self-improvement.
Some things are simply not possible.

But even so, give me tasks to do.
Let me play a part in what lovely work
might yet be.

Show me how goodness grows
in the body that I now inhabit,
within the walls of circumstance,
in these short years and finite strength,
and with these eyes that see only so far.

Give me courage to imagine
that any grand work of yours
can fit in the small space that is my life.
Show me your plans.
Sign me up.

God, I have little hope for anything more
except that you can make space here
for growing.
Right here,
where the dust has settled
on the foundations
of my well-laid plans.

for when you're sick but have no answers

Yours is the body that bears the burden,
the heart that carries the disappointment
    when operations are unsuccessful
    when medications cause side effects,
        —or don't work at all.

Yours is the life being dominated by an illness
that shouts so loudly, but in a language no one seems to understand.
Yours is the arrival that causes the consternation of experts,
the discomfort of friends, and the heartache of family.

Blessed are you, dear one,
    for you are not the problem nor the cause.
    You are everyone's reminder that terrible things do happen,
    and can keep on happening, with no end in sight.

You who are trying to hold it all—
the pain and grief and disappointments that keep coming—
when you try to protect others from their own worst fears,
to spare them the hard truths.
Blessed are you, dear heart, for you can set that burden down.
For it is ours too and we embrace it.

For we are the ones who are blessed
to receive the privilege of being with you in it,
of knowing you, seeing you, loving you, and saying with you,
Yes, life is exactly this hard,
exactly this uncertain, this fragile, this precious.
This is real.

for when you thought you would feel different by now

God, I thought I would feel
different by now,
but new pressures just keep mounting.
I have been struggling for too long
    to meet each new challenge,
    to scrape up resources,
    to find small comforts,
    to change strategies,
    to dig deep into my reserves,
    to stay positive,
but I need relief
and fresh hope
and a minute to just say,
I really wish things were easier.

**"We do not know what to do,
but our eyes are on you."**
—2 Chronicles 20:12, NIV

Just when we thought
we could almost be done with this,
another shoe drops.
There are no finish lines.
We long for the simple joys
of times past,
those everyday pleasures
we can barely remember,
but still hunger for.
A great night's sleep.
Less financial stress.
The ease of making future plans.

Blessed are we who look to you, God,
in the midst of troubles
that are too great for us,
that have gone on far too long.
Who dare to say,
Now would be a good time

for help to come,
for this to be over, once and for all.
God, send us help.
Bring solutions for the desperate,
protection for the vulnerable,
comfort for the suffering,
strength to the caregivers,
wisdom to those in charge.

God, sustain us and orient us
to the reality in which we now live.
Help us pace ourselves.
Keep us awake
to what might be done, right now.

**"I will strengthen you and help you;
I will uphold you with my righteous right hand."**
—Isaiah 41:10, NIV

68

for when you feel stuck

†

"I do not understand the mystery of grace— only that it meets us where we are and does not leave us where it found us."

—Anne Lamott,
Traveling Mercies

God, I am in the wrong place, and I know it.
But I can't get out.

Blessed are the poor in spirit,
ready to say: I have no idea how I got here,
or how to escape this stagnant place,
but I do know I am ready for
more light, more truth, more grace.

God, let there be moments today that move me
to where love and beauty can reach me.
Remind me of that deeper truth
that animates each step.

Lead me to where I can grow
and send down roots into truth I can trust,
to where love lives
and beauty is awake.

Let your heart seek the one good step.
And the next.
Movement.
That is the way.

**"You cannot think a spiritual muddle clear,
you have to obey it clear."**
—Oswald Chambers, *My Utmost for His Highest*

69

for when you feel lonely

God, there is a space here
in my heart, in my life,
I wish others could fill.

Would it be embarrassing to admit
that I'm lonely?

I need someone walking with me,
        whose eyes see what mine do,
        whose ears are open to hear my thoughts,
        and whose heart can be cracked open
        a smidge more.

I was not built to do this alone.

I feel it in the transitions, God,
in the moments I need someone to call,
after a memory I don't want to forget.
It feels like leaning back
without knowing if I will feel
the comfortable weight
of being held.

Could you remind me first that I am loved?
That my needs aren't too much.
That my personality isn't too absurd.
That the details of my life deserve a record,
kept by another.

Give me courage to look in new places,
to risk reaching out,
making plans with acquaintances
who might turn into friends.

Give me peace.
Give me hope.
Give me people.
And, in the meantime,
remind me that lovely moments
are still ahead.

bless the lives of others

70
for others

Oh God, we are surrounded by our loves.
They need you. And we need you to carry *them*.
Let love bear up the weight of us all.

Bless our kids and grandkids.
Children here and those gone.
Bless the people who quicken our hearts,
now and years past.
Bless our parents and grandparents,
strengthen our roots and our branches.
Bless our pets and your creation,
and the comfort they bring.
Bless our friends and chosen families,
all the bonds that hold us.

Thank you for this love,
this absurd and wonderful love.

God, bless the memories we hold
of those who have died,
and release in us the fullness of being able
to love them as they were in this life,
and as they are now
in the mystery that is beyond our sight.

God, bless all the people in pain who share
this present time and space with us,
whose lives are yet an unwritten book,
just like ours.
Come and write your words of love
that we speak—in our words and our actions—
in ways that heal our past
and stir up hope for our future.

God, I will openly admit
that my plan was to rescue us all.
Pry this out of my hands.
Absolve my guilt.
Calm my spirit.
Let me allow you to do the impossible
and bear up the weight of the world
I am determined to carry alone.

**"Those who refresh others
will be enriched,
and one who waters
will themself be refreshed."**
—Proverbs 11:25, NLT (paraphrased)

for when so many are suffering (and you don't know what to do)

---

†

Oh God, so many are suffering
beyond what they can bear.
Come quickly
with help that is stronger than death.

You see the vulnerable,
who face what we find hard to imagine.
And their caregivers and healthcare workers,
families, teachers, and helpers of every kind
who string together scarce resources
while they're running on empty.

"Praise be to the God . . . of all comfort, who
comforts us in all our troubles, so that we can
comfort those in any trouble with the comfort
we ourselves receive from God."
—2 Corinthians 1:3–4, NIV

Blessed are we,
still in our relative ease,
still jars of clay,
yet broken,
who give to others
what we yet can give,
who pray,
boldly,
and love fiercely.

This is the very ground of our being—
God's love for us and love working through us.

God, have mercy.
Christ, have mercy.
Spirit, have mercy.
Amen.

72

for the ones who choose
to break their hearts for ours

---

†

"Compassion constitutes a radical form of criticism, for it announces that the hurt is to be taken seriously, that the hurt is not to be accepted as normal and natural but is an abnormal and unacceptable condition for humanness."

—Walter Brueggemann, *The Prophetic Imagination*

Blessed are you who let your heart break.

    You don't have to.

    You could just have easily skirted the issue,

    shrugged it off as someone else's job.

    But you didn't.

You gave the ride or set up the meal train or sat in the waiting room.

You handed your precious time over to the inefficiency and exhaustion of tragedy.

Blessed are you who show up during someone's worst day
    because it is your job.
    The healthcare worker, funeral director, foster parent, chaplain,
    social worker, pastor, lawyer, police officer, or judge.
You who have not allowed yourself to be hardened by all you've seen.
You who offer the gift of steady presence amid swirling chaos.

Blessed are the communities of care that surround us when we fall apart.
    Knowing we can't do this alone,
    and trusting that even if we don't have the answers
    or the right words to say or know exactly what to do,
we will continue to show up.
    Again and again and again.

Because that's what love demands: to let our hearts break, *together*.

for the ones who bear witness

Blessed are the noticers. The ones who see the story in its fullness.
Blessed are the attenders. The witness-bearers. The story-holders.
    The ones who tiptoe to the edge right alongside us,
      knowing that the very act will break their heart in pieces too.
        Choosing us anyway.

Blessed are those who are amazed by a life lived
in its fragility, in its brevity, in its beauty.

Blessed are the ones who stand close enough to say: "BEHOLD."

Behold, this is their love.
Behold, this is their annoying habit.
Behold, these are the people they loved and know so much about
that they could implicate or exonerate them in a crime.

Behold, these are their exes and their favorite songs to belt out in the car, and their fast-food orders.

Behold. This is not a problem to be solved. This is a person to be loved. This is the miracle we get to call by name.

And how lucky are we?

These people.
These loves.
These precious, precious, precious days.
Thanks be to God.

"Death always thinks of us eventually. The trick is to find the joy in the interim, and make good use of the days we have."
—Ann Patchett, *These Precious Days*

74

for those who keep watch over the sick

Sometimes love alone isn't enough.
> It can't save them, save us,
> save the life we had together.
> We are finite.
> And so much is out of our control.

So bless the ones with the courage to walk all the
> way to the edge,
> > who peer over the cliff . . .
> > and feel the updraft of the abyss,
> > and who will do it all over again tomorrow.

Blessed are the hospital-room organizers
and question-askers
and the *more-ice-chips-please* gatherers.
The *absolutely, yes, this hard-backed chair is
> perfectly comfortable* sleepers
and over-the-top pray-ers and
weekly-infusion-companioners.

Blessed are the cool-cloth bringers
and the wake-up-to-get-the-meds alarmists
and the *I-don't-mind-taking-you-to-the-
> bathroom* carriers,
guarding others from their own humiliation.

Blessed are the ones who stand,
unblinking into the truth.

> No matter how terrifying,
> no matter how life-altering.
> No matter how inconvenient or unbecoming.
> No matter how much it costs them.

Because *that* is the kind of love that sticks.

Blessed are the hand-holders and truth-carriers,
for they will walk us to the end
before they have to let go.

for when loving your enemy seems too big of an ask

---

†

**"Darkness cannot drive out darkness;
only Light can do that.
Hate cannot drive out hate;
only Love can do that."**
—Rev. Martin Luther King, Jr.

Lord, this anger feels so right, so just,
that loving my enemy is inconceivable.
Am I even allowed to have an enemy?
Well, too bad. I do.
(And way more than one.)

God, I don't want to,
but help me see what I need to see,
so I can do what I know
I'm supposed to do.

Blessed are we who recognize
that the divide is deep
and the enmity strong.
We are attached now to our hostilities—
not only as symbols of who we are,
but also by the values and principles
     that we uphold.

Blessed are we who ask you, God:
Help us to be faithful to your call
to love our enemies,
for your name's sake and for ours too.
Yet we ask, How is that possible?
We desire no false peace,
no imitation grace.

Where do we begin?
How do we recover civility?
Build unity?

Work together and yet
hold on to our integrity?

Show us precisely how to love those
whom we have so lately despised.
Not just humanity in general,
but these humans, in particular.
    Yes, her. And definitely him, too.

Blessed are we who say, Oh God,
Please do for us
what we cannot do for ourselves.
Give us the desire
to speak the truth in love,
to listen to each other and hear
the humanity underneath the hurt.
Give us the wisdom and skills
to communicate well
and patience that can bear up

when things get difficult.
And where we ourselves fall short,
stand in the gap for us, Lord,
just as you did at the cross.

Pray for one enemy.
Do them some small good.
Then, let it go.

**"If your enemy is hungry,
feed him;
if he is thirsty,
give him something to drink."**
—Romans 12:20, NIV

for loving someone
when differences divide us

God, this is a hard one.
How do I begin to love or even connect
with someone so different from me?
How do I bridge this gap?
It feels just as wrong as the beliefs I abhor.

Blessed are we who want to be a part
of the wild and beautiful experiment
to find a common humanity.
Who desire to come willingly into the gap
that separates human from human,
to love the stranger—
> especially the one we really don't understand
> and secretly want to set straight.

Blessed are we, willing to stay in the gap,
in the contradictions of what we can't understand.
To actively work on disproving
our own intuitions about another,
in order to begin to see what they see.

Blessed are we, swimming upstream
against the current of our own human frailty,
our fears and emotions,
and willing to be wrong for a second.
To reconsider. And hold to our integrity
with kindness.

Desiring to see the lay of the land
and play the course,
instead of the one we wished it could be.
And to discover that humility
is what makes change possible.

Grace is never neutral.
It works backwards and forwards in time,
conspiring to make wrong right.

"We don't have time
to judge them, because
if we judge them we
don't have time to love
them."
—Rachael, a nurse, as told to
 author Christie Watson

"This is what our
Scriptures come to
teach:
in everything,
in every circumstance,
do to others as you
would have them
do to you."
—Matthew 7:12, The Voice

for the givers who need to receive

Oh God, you see them,
the ones who are overwhelmed—
the caregivers and healthcare workers,
the teachers and parents,
the first responders and chaplains,
the social workers and therapists,
all those who are givers
whose greatest need now
is simply to be able to receive.

God, come in power,
come in tenderness,
to bring them the help
and relief they need.

Blessed are those who work
so hard for so long,
struggling to shore up
the damage from hardship,
isolation, sickness, and want.
They have given
and given and given,
yet the needs keep coming.

And God, sometimes
there really is nothing extra,
no more resources,
no last-minute reprieve,
and the suffering goes on.
And what they can offer is not enough.

**"Be sure that nothing you do for God
is ever lost or ever wasted."**
—1 Corinthians 15:58, Phillips (paraphrased)

Oh God, you see that helper
who is alone
in the work and the responsibility,
in the shifting of all that rubble,
the clearing away
of the debris of calamity.
God, you see them
beginning to weaken,
beginning to collapse on the inside
from the cost on their families,
from the burnout they feel.

God, send actual support in human
    form,
to bring all that they need for rest
and the renewed resilience
that will make it possible
to fulfill the beautiful purposes
to which they are called.

And blessed are we
who consider well
how to play our part too.

Be blessed to receive.
Then find that giver
whose strength is low.
And be blessed to give.

for your great, big, dumb heart

✝

Love can break your heart. *It's probably in the fine print.*
Didn't you click the box at the bottom of the terms and conditions?

Blessed are you when your kids are ungrateful,
when your parents are unbearable,
or when they *would have been* if they were still around.
When you help an unfixable friend,
listen much longer than a normal person should,
     or give selflessly out of meager resources.

Blessed is your terrible evaluation of who is worth it.
Your cost-benefit analysis would be the laughingstock of any economist.

You ignored the signs: *Will this make you richer? Happier? Well rested?*
     Probably not.

You have been noticing for a while
how these small moments—the privilege of wrapping a blanket
around this love, that friendship, this stranger—are impossible to quantify.

Love is adding up to so much more, somehow.

Because blessed are you whose heart has grown three sizes.
 Regardless.
 You who push through
   the fear of intimacy,
   the fear of loss,
   the fear of all the unknowns,
    and choose to love still.

Blessed are we,
 loving beyond our limits,
 loving when it doesn't make sense,
 loving without any lifetime guarantees,
 loving when it might break our hearts.

That is, of course, the best thing about us: our great, big, dumb hearts.

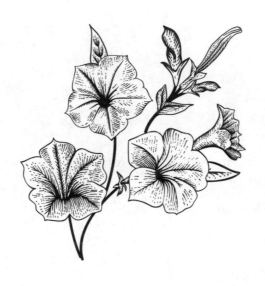

bless this
<u>beautiful</u>,
<u>limited life</u>

79

for this beautiful, limited day

†

Blessed are we who see the impossibility
of solving today.
It can't be done.

God, there are lists on lists
and errands on errands
and a taste, like tin in my mouth,
of the unfinishedness of my life.

Am I counting items
instead of knowing what counts?

God, help me live here,
seeing the whole truth of what is.

Blessed are we who walk toward the discomfort,
bringing what gifts we have,
and our sufferings too,
whether of illness or loss,
grief or betrayal,
confusion or powerlessness.

Blessed are we who scoot up close
so we can whisper our loves, our fears,
all that feels too heavy to carry alone,
and all that we wish we could hold onto for longer.

Show me what I love.
Show me what I never want to lose.
Show me what I no longer need
here in this beautiful, limited day.

for learning to delight again

✝

"Joy is a mystery because it can happen anywhere, anytime, even under the most unpromising circumstances, even in the midst of suffering, with tears in its eyes."
—Frederick Buechner, *The Hungering Dark*

Blessed are you, the pragmatic,
you who have run the math and know what adds up—and what doesn't.
You who have set it all down.
You who don't hope or dream or plan anymore
       . . . because what's the point?

Your world has shrunk.
Pain or grief or fear has sucked up every bit of oxygen from the room
    and every ounce of delight has been squeezed from your hands.
Blessed are you learning to live here,
in this unrecognizable, unnamable place.

Blessed are you who discover that even in the smallness,
    your attention might be compressed even more.

You who pull out a magnifying glass
      to discover, to notice, to taste, to smell
            the small joys and simple pleasures that make a life worth living.
You who wear the fancy blouse because it makes you feel nice
long after you thought your body wasn't worth decorating.
You who eat the over-the-top meal, because that is what today can afford.
You who make the memory and plan the trip and snap a picture because you know
    that this one wild and precious life might cost you everything.

So why not make it not just bearable—but *beautiful*?

P.S. If you want to read a gorgeous poem, go look up Mary Oliver's "The Summer Day" and her beautiful question: "What is it you plan to do with your one wild and precious life?" And she says it is about DOING NOTHING. So we can all chill out.

for when you need to hold on or let go

God, sometimes it feels like a better person wouldn't be like this:
     tethered to so many hopes,
     and fears, and expectations.

Blessed are we pulled between wanting to let go
—sometimes needing to let go—and also needing to hold on.

Blessed are we when we yearn
     for connection and love and touch.

Blessed are we when we hunger
     for the beauty of life itself and the people to fill it.

Blessed are we when we are unable to say,
     "I'm letting it go."
     Because we feel like we will be washed away into an ocean of nothingness.

Teach us to cling to the truths that enliven our spirits,
    and loosen our grip on the painful untruths:
        like the one that says we are alone, or unlovable.
        Or that desire itself is the enemy.
Teach us to hunger for what is good, and be filled.

There will be no easy addition and subtraction.
    We will lose and we will gain,
    and almost none of it will make much sense at the time,
    and it will force our hands open.
In the ebb and flow of wins and losses, comings and goings,
    may we look for the divine in the mystery of it all,
    the stubbornness of flowers that still smile at us in the grocery store,
    and the need for endless small reminders
        that the pain of it all, the comedy of it all,
        will point us back to love.

for an unfinishable day

†

God, it seems that stopping is impossible.
Dishes need to be washed.
Kids need to be fed.
Aging parents need to be cared for.
Deadlines need to be met.
Medicines need to be administered.
Diapers always need to be changed.
(They multiply if I sleep, after all.)

Can you ease the burden of perfection?
Free me from this fantasy
of the better me—
my new exercise regime,
my sumptuous (healthy!) new recipes,
the way the perfect placement
of my living room furniture
would flatter the afternoon light
on my social media feed.

God, make me more than perfect.
Make me more than a job or role,
or what I had planned for my golden years.

Make me something less predictable
than my to-do lists
and daily calendar.

In this culture of more, more, more,
make me less.

Less tidy and afraid,
less polished and buttoned up,
less prideful and judgmental.

Turn down the volume of my expectations,
and let me hear the birds sing
another lovely truth:

I am deeply and wholly loved.
I am beautiful and somehow delightful
even as I am *unfinished*.

for beginnings and endings

†

This life is made up of so many
  beginnings and so many endings.
We start new jobs and leave old ones.
We move to new cities and leave our
  childhood hobbies in our parents'
  basement. (Sorry, Mom.)
We become new people slowly
  (hopefully kinder and funnier?).
Friends and relationships
  come and go.
Dreams blossom and then they wither.

And we find ourselves here once again
at the precipice of change.
Afraid to let go,
and afraid of what will happen if we
  don't.
Might this be a place of blessing too?

Blessed are we standing in the hallway
  between closed doors
  and ones still to come,
  between the old and the new,
  between the worn-in
  and the doesn't-quite-yet-fit,
  between who we were
  and who we might become.

God, make it remotely possible
to grow and change,
become open to new adventures, and
untethered to routine
or to the same-old.
Because the anxiety rising in my
  shoulders and filling my throat
tells me I am unlikely, unwilling,
to step forward.

Blessed are we who take a minute
to look over our shoulder
at all we learned from what was,
the people we became,
the people who loved us into becoming.
The peace that came with familiarity.

Blessed are we who trust this timing,
and who open our hearts anew
to change, to new friends, to hope.
Nervous, maybe heavy-hearted,
but brimming with gratitude for a life
so beautiful that it hurts to say
    goodbye.

Blessed are we, turning our eyes ahead
toward a new path not yet mapped.
God, give us courage to take this
    next step,

and enough for the one after that, too.
Remind us that you have gone before,
and behind, and around,
and are with us now.

In our leaving, in our arriving,
in our changes, expected or shocking,
surprise us with who we might
    become.

for the courage to do something difficult

"I took courage, for the hand of the Lord my God was on me."
—Ezra 7:28, ESV

God, I am struggling to face the difficult thing I know I should do.
The conversation I've been avoiding.
The help I should have asked for months ago.
The symptom I have long ignored.

Oh God, help me.
I am afraid to act,
but afraid to admit my inaction
might be making things worse.

Blessed are we who recognize that
we are struggling under the weight
of the nothing that has happened
but needs to.

**"But when I am afraid,
I will put my trust in you."**
—Psalm 56:3, NLT

Blessed are we who say honestly,
God, this is so hard, and I don't know why.
The longer I leave it, the worse it gets.

God, help me begin—or even begin to begin—
though I can't know how this will go.
Fill that inner space
where I am quietly overwhelmed
and stuck in mud. Or maybe it's quicksand.

I hear you say: "I will strengthen you and help you." (Isaiah 41:10, NIV)
You go before me
and you are right here with me. Even now.
In my panicking, in my anxieties, in my master-avoidance.
Your love never fails.

P.S. Do the thing you've been putting off. Right now. Take the first small step.
Make the appointment. Schedule the meeting. Check your bank account.
Tell a friend you are struggling. Then ask for what you need next.

85

for when you want more

†

God, I carry around this incompleteness,
this drive for fulfillment that always seems
just around the corner.
If only I could get it together and
find my true calling, my real passion,
or the right plan.
God, help me, guide me. What am I missing?

Blessed are we who strive earnestly
to change ourselves and the world around us,
but feel the drag and pull of what won't budge,
the weight of all our limited and frail humanity.
We carry it with us.

Blessed are we, the hungry,
in lives that are both too much and not enough,
willing to tell the truth to ourselves
and to each other,
that we languish here . . .
in what is perhaps the central paradox
of our condition—

that "what we hunger for perhaps more than
    anything else
is to be known in our full humanness,
and yet that is often just what we also
fear more than anything else."*

To be fully known, and fully loved,
in all our humanity.
That is a God-sized project.

Blessed are we, thankful that we can live
our human-sized lives
in the glad company of the vulnerable
and the broken,
the imperfect made whole in the love of God,
through Jesus Christ.
Maybe it's right to be hungry. And stay that way.

* Frederick Buechner, *Telling Secrets,*
  (New York: HarperCollins, 1991).

86

for the life you didn't choose

†

Blessed are you when the shock subsides,
when vaguely, you see a line appear
that divides before and after.

You didn't draw it,
and can barely even make it out.
But as surely as minutes add up to hours and days,
here you are,
forced into a story you never would have written.

Blessed are you in the tender place
of awe and dread,
wondering how to be whole
when dreams have disappeared
and part of you with them,
where mastery, control, determination,
bootstrapping, and grit
are consigned to the realm of Before
(where most of the world lives),
in the fever dream that promises infinite choices,
unlimited progress, best life now.

Blessed are we in the After zone, loudly shouting:
Is there anybody here?
We hear the echo, the shuffle of feet,
the murmur of others
asking the same question,
together in the knowledge
that we are far beyond what we know.

God, show us a glimmer of possibility
in this new constraint,
that small truths will be given back to us.
>We are held.
>We are safe.
>We are loved.
>We are loved.
>We are loved.

for who you might become

"You have made us
and drawn us to yourself,
and our heart is restless
until it rests in you."
—Augustine of Hippo,
   The Confessions of St. Augustine

God, I'm haunted by the shadows
of the old me.
The one who's tried every
promised elixir, every five-step plan,
every guru's solution to what ails me.
But nothing seems to stick.

I'm the same me
with the same problems
and the same quiet hopes.

Is it my lack of discipline?
Or am I just a lost cause?
What new beginnings are possible?

Blessed are we, the incomplete,
standing at the edge of what could be,
in this perpetual season of waiting
and looking and longing
for the fulfillment of hope.

Blessed are we, the restless,
grieving what's over, but isn't done,
what is gone, but isn't finished.

Blessed are we,
in our midnight struggle with past
and future,
while the present has already arrived
outside our door

like flat-packed furniture
with missing parts.

God, what can we do
with what we have now?
And who we are?
And who might we become?

Blessed are we in the place
where desire and will
are beginning a conversation
about what this day,
this moment is for,
and for whose glory.

Blessed are we who suddenly find
that while we weren't looking,
the Lord appeared saying,
"Peace, be still."

This is the clearing
where the light shines through,
where the new can begin.

Never doubt it.
God is writing you into the story
of the world's healing.
And your own.

**"From now on I will tell you
of new things, of hidden things
unknown to you."**
—Isaiah 48:6, NIV

88

for the good already come (and gone)

People like to say, "The best is yet to come,"
as some sort of guarantee.
Could we say, perhaps, lovingly
    (or angrily, if we feel like it):
    "Sometimes the best isn't ahead"?
We lose things, jobs, abilities . . . people.

Sometimes we have crescendoed.
Sometimes the best has already come.

Blessed are you who have finished humming
the tune of parenthood,
because you didn't have that baby
or they've grown up and out.
You who are playing the closing notes
of a parent's life,
or a friend's, or a child's.
You who are retiring or
moving out of the home you loved
or from the place that made you *you.*

Blessed are you who still have
much to sing about—

new hobbies and loves and friends and hopes.
You who wonder how best
to spend your time, efforts, resources, and gifts
exactly *because* they are in short supply.

You who know to keep the end in mind.

Blessed are we, who see with such crisp clarity
the gift that was, and that is,
and that might yet be.
Knowing—really knowing—that someday,
the last note will be sung.

So let's sing our songs about our beautiful,
ridiculous lives.
We will peak and crescendo and
approach the finale,
hoping for a pretty damn good finish.

bless this
holy life

Bless This Lent

WHAT IS LENT?

Lent marks the forty days leading up to Easter, mirroring the forty days Jesus spent in the wilderness. It is a practice that began during the fourth century as a way to prepare Christians for the holiest days of the year.

During Lent, we ask God to show us the world as it is. We begin with the reality of our finitude rubbed on our foreheads on Ash Wednesday—from dust we were made, to dust we shall return. Then, we walk through that reality in a kind of dress rehearsal. It's the downward slope of God—the Great Descent, where the whole church walks toward the cross.

Frankly, Lent is my favorite part of the church calendar, because it is a time when the whole church is on the losing team. A time when we all get a minute to tell the truth: Life is so beautiful and life is so hard. For everyone.

Of course, the cross isn't the end of the story, but this season of grief is carved out to acknowledge the reality of Christ's sacrifice. And the reality of suffering that so many of our circumstances reflect too—our own pain and grief and despair. Easter is coming, yes. But for now, we sit in the ashes of our broken dreams and broken hearts, knowing that God sits here with us.

Many people practice Lent by giving something up—alcohol, meat, chocolate, social media. Some take up something new—a new prayer practice or swearing profusely, like I did one year. [You probably remember reading about this in *Everything Happens for a Reason (and Other Lies I've Loved)*.]

But Lent is an incredible moment for the spiritual honesty we are practicing here. Together, we're going to bless the days we have, while longing for the future God promised, when there will be no tears, no pain, no email.

We have selected forty blessings that you might use on the forty days of Lent (as well as Sundays during the Lenten season). Each is denoted by a small cross on that page's entry.

If you are looking to go deeper, we've put together an additional Lenten reflection guide as a companion to this book. We're calling it "Bless This Lent," and it's available anytime on my website at katebowler.com/BlessThisLent. This free guide includes scriptures to read, discussion questions, and a place to reflect on the journey through Lent to Easter.

Whether you are practicing Lent solo or using this book with your church, in a book club, or around the dinner table with your family, you can anchor your days using the following handpicked blessings—or find even more richness and depth by using them along with the accompanying reflection guide.

A NOTE ON SUNDAYS

Lent lasts for a full forty days, but Sundays don't count. They are mini-Easters, where we take a day off from whatever we are abstaining from, days to remind us that we are made for both—grief and joy, sorrow and delight. Strangely, this might feel like a hard thing to do—to make yourself stop working or worrying or checking off your day's reading—*and really rest.*

But over the next six weeks, you're invited to press against that part of your wiring that tells you that you must always be accomplishing, producing, processing—that everything must be *for* something. And take a day off from the Lent-y feelings to practice the discipline of Sabbath. Rest! Eat! Enjoy!

for Ash Wednesday

†

"Ash Wednesday is full of joy . . . The source of all sorrow is the illusion that of ourselves we are anything but dust."

—Thomas Merton, *The Sign of Jonas*

God, today my finitude is rubbed on my forehead.
The reality of my limits, my fragile body,
spoken over me like a curse:
from dust I was made
        to dust I will return.

Some days I need to be reminded
that I am not the perfectibility project
I set out to be.
I am full of bounce and brimming with hope.
All woes, solvable. All problems, a distant whisper.
When I don't feel like dust,
Bless me, oh God,
in the ways I trick myself into believing
that my life is something I've made,
that all my accomplishments and successes
and mastered mornings
add up to something independent of you.

But on days like today, when my head hangs low,
sunk with the grief of my neediness,
Bless me, oh God.
When my joints don't work like they should,
when I grow sick or turn gray too soon,
when my body betrays me . . .
or perhaps it is doing exactly
what it is supposed to do.
Tell me again
exactly how you made me:
     from dust to dust.

Blessed are we, a mess of contradictions,
in our delusions and deep hopes,
in our fragility and finitude.

for Palm Sunday

✝

**"Blessed are those who have learned
to . . . walk in the light of your presence."**
—Psalm 89:15, NIV

Oh God, you are interrupting me with eternity.
And I'm not sure I'm ready.

Take hold of time and order it once again.
Let me keep pace with you.

On this Palm Sunday, time is marked as one small donkey
    plods toward Jerusalem.
One with a face set like flint, feet almost grazing the ground, walks forward
    toward the eastering of all sorrow
        —not in the power of horses and swift victory,
           but in small, steady steps
    toward the mystery
        that through suffering, healing comes,

that through shame, dignity is restored,
that through the cross, powers are disarmed,
and death done away with forever.

Blessed are all those walking forward
into the great, small work they do:
in hospitals, homes, grocery stores,
classrooms, churches, and cubicles.

And blessed are we joining the crowds
waving palm branches
to shout ourselves hoarse:
"Hosanna! Save us! Save our world."

God, have mercy. Christ, have mercy. Spirit, have mercy. Amen.

for Maundy Thursday

✝

This is the night that it begins,
the festival of grief and somehow triumph.
The end is near.

Jesus, we are beginning to understand that
your grace makes no sense—
grace sits next to betrayers,
grace washes the feet of backstabbers,
grace breaks bread with the disloyal,
grace shares a cup with double-dealers.

Jesus, you are undoing every guarantee
that, in loving you, I will not lose.

You are losing everything.

Bless me now, as I see your sacrifice.
How you are pleading with us to love,
as your friends break your heart.
How you are showing us how to remember,
when we long to forget
that in your undoing, you remade the world.

for Good Friday

"The light shines in the darkness, and the darkness has not overcome it."
—John 1:5, NIV

Oh dear God, we are in darker places
    than we've ever known,
    than we ever wanted to be.

Our usual strategies of coping
aren't working.
    We are lost.
    We are afraid.
    We are fresh out of answers.

Oh God, light the way
    for this whole heart-heavy earth,
    for the helpless and hopeless,
    for those drowning in grief
    or fear or depression,
    for the tired and harried
    and the at-the-end-of-their-rope,
    for those weary of their sins
    and those who aren't,
    and for me, too.

God, have mercy.
Christ, have mercy.
Spirit, have mercy.

The thick of dusk has fallen
    and betrayal seems
    the order of the day.

The night when Love itself
was handed over
    to brutal ignorance
    and cunning that loves deceit.

Oh God, you chose to feel
what we feel—
    to be spit on, ridiculed, tortured,
    and to die all alone.
    In your outstretched arms
    on the cross,
        are you gathering to
          yourself
        every hideous thing,
        every failure, travesty,
        and wrong?

Blessed are we who say:
Yes! Take this pain.
    Turn things right side up again.
    I can see, only now,
    that you will follow me to the end
    and beyond.

The day love died,
something new was born,
and may we be a people,
open to the grief, the loss,
and then, yes,
    the rising of the Son.

for Holy Saturday

†

Oh God, there are no more answers.
> Only silence,
> and the echoes of yesterday's questions.

God, have mercy.
Christ, have mercy.
Spirit, have mercy.

Oh God, soften my heart to be able to mourn
what is lost.
> Help me to name it now.
>> The people I thought I couldn't live
>> without.
>> The hope I can no longer conjure.
>> The joy that used to come quickly.

Oh God, unbind this sorrow.
> Let me lament and cry and tremble,
>> for one lies broken—
>> poured out and spent,
>>> entombed.

I want to listen in the quiet of this small space
    and wait
        until I get used to the dark.
So I can see the cracks
in the foundations of the world
    left by the thunder of your passing,
to see all the ragged truth of what is,
to touch and feel and love and
hold the edges of what was,
to honor what is forever gone.

And to love well
what is eternally given.

**"Blessed are those
who mourn,
for they shall be
comforted."**
—Matthew 5:4, ESV

for Easter Sunday

†

"On the evening of that day, the first day of the week . . . Jesus came and stood among them and said to them, *Peace be with you."*

—John 20:19, ESV

Oh God, I stretch out my hands to you
in this early Easter darkness.
I need you to pull me up
and set me on my feet again,
for I am weak and tired.

God, have mercy.
Christ, have mercy.
Spirit, have mercy.

God, on that first Easter morning
while it was still dark,
one woman went alone to the tomb
to do what could be done to honor you,
    though hope had drained away.

Two bright angels met her there, and then—
    how is it possible?—

you were there, fully alive, beyond belief.

Blessed are we who stretch out our hands to you
      in doubt and grief,
      in sickness of body and mind and spirit,
      our prayers not fully realized,
      rejoicing . . . anyway.

For that is what makes us Easter people:
      carrying forth the realized hope
      of the Resurrected One,
      singing our alleluias great and small,
         while it is still dark.

Christ is risen. Christ will come again.

Alleluia. Alleluia. Alleluia.

Bless This Advent

WHAT IS ADVENT

Advent is that special time of year leading up to Christmas. The season is roughly four weeks before Christmas (the actual number of days varies every year), and it acts like a long dawn. We are preparing for a great inversion: God coming to Earth in the form of a human baby. The ruler of the cosmos trapped in a squalling package of helpless flesh. He was born to save us—and he will—but first he must melt our hearts, appearing not as a sage or a philosopher or an emperor, but as a cold little child with nowhere to call home. He disarms us with his tender vulnerability and summons us to enter his world as little children too.

For many, this is where the story ends: a gentle knock on the door of the human heart. This tender moment of conscience is well-suited to acts of charity, which allow people to keep their roles: giver and receiver, rich and poor, high and low, immigrant and local, white and Black, police and policed. A tiny blip in our normal consumerism and capitalism.

But Christmas beckons believers to see the kingdom of God through a starker disruption of the ordinary. "The last will be first" (Matthew 20:16, NIV). "I was a stranger and you welcomed me" (Matthew 25:35, ESV). "He has brought down rulers from their thrones but has lifted up the humble" (Luke 1:52, NIV).

We want this. We are hungry for the world turned upside down, which is precisely what Christmas has been all throughout Christian history. Medieval Western Europe allotted Christmas days to different groups at the margins of society— servants, old women, young girls, and children—allowing them to step forward and demand charity from their masters. The magic of this time of year was a moment of suspension (if temporary) of business as usual. These moments pointed to the clues everywhere that powers—oppressive and pervasive powers—rule this world. And for eleven months we fail to see them as they really are.

We all see the world as it has always been. And we are all waiting with bated breath for the kingdom of God to break in.

And in the meantime, we need to bless the days we have, the shorter days and endless nights. The experience of hope and the fear of disappointment. This is the season for all of us who need that extra hour of darkness, preferably under a blanket near the tree, to feel the immensity of what we've gained and what we've lost.

Our hope is that these blessings for each of the Sundays of Advent will be a way for you to make the very act of waiting holy. And as we anticipate Christ's birth together, may we experience the stubborn hope of Christmas, joy in the midst of sorrow, a love that knows no bounds, and a transcendent peace amid a world on fire.

If you are looking to go deeper this Advent, we've put together an Advent guide to be a companion to this book. We're calling it "Bless This Advent," and it's available anytime on my website at katebowler.com/BlessThisAdvent. This free guide includes devotional entries, scriptures to read, discussion questions, and a place to reflect on the journey to Advent.

If you are reflecting on this season on your own or with a group, we hope you can use this reflection guide to feel surrounded with love during this season.

for the first Sunday of Advent—hope

God, these are darkening days, with little hope in sight.
Help us in our fear and exhaustion. Anchor us in hope.

Blessed are we with eyes open to see the accumulated suffering of danger,
    sickness, and loneliness,
        the injustice of racial oppression,
        the unimpeded greed and misuse of power, violence, intimidation,
        and use of dominance for its own sake,
        the mockery of truth,
        and disdain for weakness or vulnerability
            —and worse, the seeming powerlessness of anyone trying to stop it.

Blessed are we who ask:
    Where are you, God?
            And where are your people
            —the smart and sensible ones who fight for good
            and have the power to make it stick?

Blessed are we who cry out: Oh God, why does the bad always seem to win?
When will good prevail? We know you are good, but we see so little goodness.

God, show us your heart,
how you seek out the broken.
Lift us on your shoulders,
and carry us home—no matter how strong we think we are.

God, seek us out, and find us, we your tired people,
and lead us out to where hope lies,
where your kingdom will come
and your will be done, on earth as it is in heaven.

Fill us with your courage.
Calm us with your love.
Fortify us with your hope.

P.S. Open your hands as you release your prayers.
Then take hold of hope. As protest.

**"Let not your heart be troubled;
you believe in God, believe also in Me."**
—John 14:1, NKJV

for the second Sunday of Advent—love

**"Are you the one who is to come,
or shall we look for another?"**
—Matthew 11:3, ESV

God, we are waiting for love,
not the simple kind or the sweep-you-off-your-feet
   kind,
but the absurd kind.

The kind wrapped in rags,
resting in a bucket of animal feed.
Love enough to save us all.

Blessed are we who look for Love
      deeper, fuller, truer—than we have ever
         known,
            than we could have ever hoped for.

Blessed are we who seek you,
the light that dawned so long ago
in that dark stable.
Love given.
Love received.

Receive this gift, dear one.
Love has come for you.

97

for the third Sunday of Advent—joy

Blessed are we who wait with bated breath,
 who wait for something new to be born
  —for new hope or new joy or new life.

Blessed are we whose patience grows thinner
by the day.
 We who are tired of the world as it is
  —in all of its heartache and loss
  and hopelessness.
 We who want more.
  More hope. More joy. More life.

Blessed are we who sit here,
 waiting at the still point between desire
 and expectation.
 We who are making room for more of you,
 oh God, this Christmas.

Surprise us with joy in the midst of the mundane,
abundance in the midst of so much scarcity,
presence in the midst of Christmas chaos.

We have quieted our souls to listen,
to wait for you, oh God,
for your Word-Made-Flesh is life to us.

Amen.

**"Now may the God of hope fill you with all joy and
peace in believing,
that you may abound in hope by the power of the
Holy Spirit."**
—Romans 15:13, NKJV

for the fourth Sunday of Advent— peace

Blessed are we, the fearful,
though we long to be people of peace.
We can't lie:
we are afraid.

Afraid there won't be enough—
enough resources,
enough time,
enough memories.

Blessed are we who ask you for wisdom.
Show us what to turn from,
what to set aside.

Come, Lord, that we might
see you,
move with you,
keep pace with you.

Blessed are we who ask that this Advent
we might dwell together quietly in our homes.
Come, Lord, that we might be for others
the peace they cannot find.

Blessed are we who look to you and say,
God, truly, we are troubled and afraid.
Come govern our hearts and calm our fears.

Oh Prince of Peace,
    still our restless selves,
    calm our anxious hearts,
    quiet our busy minds.

**"Glory to God in the
highest heaven,
and on earth peace to
those on whom his
favor rests."**
—Luke 2:14, NIV

for Christmas Eve

Jesus, this is the great inversion
I would not have known
had you not appeared and made yourself
small.

Jesus, I would have been satisfied
with the God who moves mountains
and whose breath imparts life
but who never cried in his mother's arms.

The world whispers to me about
what must be done.
About empires and war.
About efficiency and strength,
but there you are.
A refusal.

Your fragility, a witness.
Your dependence, an invitation.
Your cry, a reminder.
Our finitude is not an embarrassment,
because neither was yours.

Blessed are we when we see love,
at long last,
in every small and tender thing,
stealing into our world
to change us all.

for Christmas Day

God, this is a kind of magic
the way this day shines so strangely,
how it sparkles beyond our understanding.

(Yes, it was a disaster
the way the food turned out this year
and how what's-her-face said—I told her not to—
what shouldn't be repeated.
Again, this year.)

But, somehow, this day
never fails to awaken a longing
to love well—or at least better—
all those here with us, and those far away,
and to remember with gratitude
those now gone, gone, gone and missed.

What is this mystery?

Our God, who set the world spinning,
should come down for this one reason:
to love us into newness.
Not for gain, nor our capitalist fantasies,
but for the hope so freely, lavishly given
that we might learn to see, feel,
and live Christ's love.
Thank you,
Christ the Giver and the Gift.

Amen.

Acknowledgments

We started blessing people—everyone, for everything, all the time—right before we needed it the most. We were in the last gasps of the freedom of 2019 before the long pandemic would take over the lives we knew and loved. And suddenly, all at once, we needed a new language for the daily needs and fears that threaten to engulf us all.

This book is first and foremost for you—our Everything Happens community. You who spend your beautiful, terrible days reading our books, or listening to our podcast episodes, or praying these words of blessing. You who send in the stories of your loves and losses and pains and hopes. (We seriously read every single one.) We got weepy time and again imagining the way the words on these pages might meet you in your grief and hope and ordinary (sometimes very boring) realities. Learning to be useful to you in this way blesses us more than you know.

Thank you to Lilly Endowment, The Duke Endowment, Duke Divinity School, and Leadership Education at Duke Divinity for their ongoing support of our medium-sad work. We are so lucky.

Our imperfect days are made infinitely more bearable because we get to work alongside these people: Harriet Putman, who infuses compassion and kindness into every interaction and makes every step of this work real ministry, and Gwen Heginbotham, our very own Midas—everything she touches becomes beautiful. Keith Weston, Jeb Burt, and Sammi Filippi, who share their great gifts with us every week. Dave Odom, Katherine Smith, and Edgardo Colón-Emeric, for their wisdom and friendship. Chris Coble, Verity Jones, and Robb Webb, for always conspiring to make new projects dreamable. And this project wouldn't have been possible without the help of Karen Bowler, who takes the charge to pray without ceasing quite seriously.

Thank you to our publishing team for championing our very Jesus-y projects— Christy Fletcher, Keren Baltzer, Leita Williams, Jessalyn Foggy, Alisse Goldsmith-Wissman, Cindy Murray, Campbell Wharton, and Tina Constable.

And, Kate here: thank you to Toban and Zach. For all the gratitude I feel when I see us do all the little things I feared would never be mine. Bedtimes. Camping. Listening to a podcast about pirates. I will never unlearn what it's like to feel blessed in the ordinary dumbness of a day.

This is Jess at the keys now. :) My parents are some of the best pray-ers I know. I am who I am because of (and in spite of) the two of you. Kate and I worked on this book right as I relocated to Delaware, away from a city and from the people (especially you, Kate Bowler) that I love—a transition that would have felt impossible were it not for the Bale family. Thank you for welcoming me with wide-open hearts. Apparently, I can't believe *everything* they say about in-laws. And, of course, to the blessing I never thought I'd deserve—Christian Bale. I didn't even think to have prayed for you. Your love makes me rethink my theology a bit because, really, who could be this lucky?

ABOUT THE AUTHORS

KATE BOWLER is the *New York Times* bestselling author of *Everything Happens for a Reason (And Other Lies I've Loved)*, *No Cure for Being Human (And Other Truths I Need to Hear)*, *Good Enough: 40ish Devotionals for a Life of Imperfection*, *Blessed: A History of the American Prosperity Gospel*, and *The Preacher's Wife: The Precarious Power of Evangelical Women Celebrities*. An associate professor of American Religious History at Duke Divinity School, she earned her undergraduate degree from Macalester College, Master of Religion from Yale Divinity School, and PhD from Duke University. She founded the Everything Happens Project, a center for everyday empathy at Duke Divinity School.

KateBowler.com

@KateCBowler

JESSICA RICHIE is the coauthor of the *New York Times* bestseller *Good Enough: 40ish Devotionals for a Life of Imperfection*, the executive director of the Everything Happens Project at Duke Divinity School, and the executive producer of the Everything Happens podcast. She received her MDiv from Duke Divinity School.

@JessTRichie